the good story

Exchanges on Truth, Fiction and Psychotherapy

Also by J. M. Coetzee

J. M. Coetzee and Arabella Kurtz

the good story

Exchanges on Truth, Fiction and Psychotherapy

Harvill Secker
London

1 3 5 7 9 10 8 6 4 2

Harvill Secker, an imprint of Vintage,
20 Vauxhall Bridge Road,
London SW1V 2SA

Harvill Secker is part of the Penguin Random House group of companies
whose addresses can be found at global.penguinrandomhouse.com

Copyright © J. M. Coetzee and Arabella Kurtz 2015

J. M. Coetzee and Arabella Kurtz have asserted their right to be identified
as the authors of this work in accordance with the Copyright, Designs and
Patents Act 1988

First published by Harvill Secker in 2015

www.vintage-books.co.uk

A CIP catalogue record for this book is available from the British Library

ISBN 9781846558887 (hardback)
ISBN 9781846558894 (trade paperback)
ISBN 9781473512290 (ebook)

Typeset in Fournier MT Std/Perpetua Std by Palimpsest Book
Production Limited, Falkirk, Stirlingshire

Printed and bound in Great Britain by Clays Ltd, St Ives plc

Penguin Random House is committed to a sustainable future for our
business, our readers and our planet. This book is made from Forest
Stewardship Council® certified paper

the good story

Exchanges on Truth, Fiction and Psychotherapy

AUTHORS' NOTE

The exchanges that follow are about the practice of psycho-analytic psychotherapy and what that practice means in a wider social and philosophical sphere. They touch on psychic processes, in individuals and in groups, both inside and outside of the clinical setting. Given that in our secular age and in the Western world psychotherapy and the ideal of personal growth have become part of the Zeitgeist, we hope that they will also be felt to be relevant to readers beyond the borders of the therapeutic profession.

The exchanges are premised on the idea that something is to be gained by a therapist exploring their practice in the company of an outsider to the discipline of psychology, in this case a sympathetically disposed writer and literary critic. On the face of it the psychotherapist and the novelist have much in common, at least in terms of the focus of their interest. Human nature and human experience concern them both deeply, as do possibilities of growth and development.

Language is the working medium of both writers and psycho-therapists. Both are occupied with the exploration, description and analysis of human experience, with finding or inventing linguistic and narrative structures within which to contain experience, and with the outer limits of experience.

The intellectual engagement reflected in these exchanges commenced in 2008, and reflects (on the one side) the interest of a therapist struck by a body of novelistic work in which internal processes are conveyed from a point of view that is radically different from a psychotherapeutic one (for instance, the terse, energetic account of Michael K's mental resistance to oppression in *Life & Times of Michael K*); and (on the other side) the interest of a writer in deepening his understanding of a post-religious form of therapeutic dialogue.

This book is the second product of this engagement. The first appeared under the title 'Nevertheless, my sympathies are with the Karamazovs' in the journal *Salmagundi*, nos. 166–167 (2010), pp. 39–72.

These exchanges are offered in an interdisciplinary spirit, as well as in a spirit of exploration. They do not always follow a linear train of thought. They sometimes repeat and contradict themselves, they return to insistent preoccupations, they pursue lines of thinking without always knowing where they will lead – all of this in the hope that they may here and there open a new or unusual perspective on the practice of psychoanalytic psychotherapy and on the psychotherapeutic project in its wider social forms.

The authors wish to acknowledge the following for their

helpful comments on drafts of the exchanges and/or for valuable discussion of relevant ideas: Nick Everett, Jillian Vites, Orna Hadary, Margot Waddell and Daisy Evans.

AK & JMC

NOTE ON THE USE OF CLINICAL EXAMPLES

Details in the clinical examples used in the exchanges have been changed to protect the anonymity of patients. The option of disguising material rather than obtaining consent from patients has been chosen because of the risk of intrusion into the therapeutic process.

GLOSSARY AND REFERENCES

Terms in bold are defined in the Glossary. Asterisks direct the reader to the References.

ONE

Being author of one's life-story (inventing one's past) versus being merely its narrator. Producing a well-shaped story versus telling the true story.

The analyst as the story's ideally attentive listener. Hearing and analysing resistances in the narrative. The therapeutic goal: freeing the patient's voice, the patient's narrative imagination.

JMC – What are the qualities of a good (a plausible, even a compelling) story? When I tell other people the story of my life – and more importantly when I tell myself the story of my life – should I try to make it into a well-formed artefact, passing swiftly over the times when nothing happened, heightening the drama of the times when lots was happening, giving the narrative a shape, creating anticipation and suspense; or on the contrary should I be neutral, objective, striving to tell a kind of truth that would meet the criteria of the courtroom: the truth, the whole truth, and nothing but the truth?

What relationship do I have with my life history? Am I its conscious author, or should I think of myself as simply a voice uttering with as little interference as possible a stream of words welling up from my interior? Above all, given the wealth of material I hold in memory, the material of a lifetime, what should or must I leave out, bearing in mind Freud's warning that what I omit without thinking (i.e. without conscious thought) may be the key to the deepest truth about me? Yet how is it logically possible for me to know what I am unthinkingly leaving out?

∽

AK – I suppose it is the task of psychoanalysis to try to tell the deepest truth; or more modestly and more accurately, to analyse resistances to its telling so that an individual's story can emerge in as full and coherent and engaged a way as possible at any one point – because the process is continuous, the story ever-changing. The true story one might tell as a child will be different from the story one might tell about the same experiences as an adolescent, or an adult, and so on.

Freud proposed the method of free association as the best way of getting access to unconscious experience in the consulting room, but in my experience it really doesn't work in the way people expect. The patient is invited to speak as freely as they are able, without reference to normal social rules and niceties, but what he or she usually discovers is the extent to which free expression is constrained – even in the privacy of their own minds. What this does is allow us to see the way that **defences** operate for the individual and to work on the analysis of **resistance**, which is a substantial task in most therapies.

One way of thinking about psychoanalysis is to say that it is aimed at setting free the narrative or autobiographical imagination. If we follow this line, then it is possible that a writer like yourself may have insights to offer on the form that narrative takes in the consulting room.

∞

JMC – Very well. Then let me ask a question that has nagged at me for some time. What is it that impels you, as a therapist, to want your patient to confront the truth about themself, as opposed to collaborating or colluding in a story – let us call it a fiction, but an empowering fiction – that would make the patient feel good about themself, good enough to go out into the world better able to love and work?

A more radical way of posing the same question is: Are all autobiographies, all life-narratives, not fictions, at least in the sense that they are constructions (fiction from Latin *fingere*, to shape or mould or form)? The claim here is not that autobiography is free, in the sense that we can make up our life-story as we wish. Rather, the claim is that in making up our autobiography we exercise the same freedom that we have in dreams, where we impose a narrative form that is our own, even if influenced by forces that are obscure to us, on elements of a remembered reality.

As we are both aware, there are varieties of self-help therapy that pretty clearly see their goal as making the subject feel good about themself, and that tend to be dismissive of the criterion of truth if the truth is too much to handle. We tend to look down on such therapies. We say that the cure they produce is only a seeming cure, that sooner or later the subject will again crash against reality. Yet what if, by some kind of social consensus, we agreed not to rock the boat but on the contrary to come together to affirm one another's fantasies, as happens in some therapeutic groups? Then there would be no reality to crash against.

In our liberal, post-religious culture we tend to think of the narrative imagination as a benign force within us. But there is another way of seeing it, based on our experience of how self-narratives work in many people's lives: as a faculty we use to elaborate for ourselves and our circle the story that suits us best, a story that justifies the way we have behaved in the past and behave in the present, a story in which we are generally right and other people are generally wrong. When this self-narrative clashes blatantly with reality, with the way things really are, we as observers conclude that the subject is deluded, that the truth-for-the-self produced by the subject's imagination is in conflict with the real truth. Therefore is it not one of the duties of the therapist to bring it home to the patient that they are not free to make up their life-story, that making up stories about ourselves can have serious real-world consequences?

∽

AK — But a narrative about one's life that is too self-serving in the way you describe will have a frailty, a brittleness, a tendency to come undone on its own terms. One could describe the activity of psychoanalysis as a combination of attentive listening and selective comment — on those aspects of a life-story which do not seem to hold, or which seem to hint at the possibility that a more convincing underlying story may emerge. This is what I meant when I said that I think of psychoanalysis as aimed at freeing the narrative imagination.

I want to ask you as a writer whether this idea, that of working through mask-narratives to find a truer one, resonates? I mean truer in the sense of poetic or emotional truth, when a thing is both true to itself, internally coherent, and in correspondence with things outside, but not necessarily in a way that is transparent or direct. And what writers know, and psychotherapists can learn from them I believe, is that the best way of trying to get to something both true and new, or newly conscious, is often a creative one; or at least at odds with what is established and laid down as true in an unexamined way in our communal, shared reality.

I do believe that the better psychotherapists, like the better and more sympathetic listeners, attend more to the internal coherence of a narrative — the unspoken desires and frustrations, which emerge gradually in inconsistencies and disruptions of form and content — and impose less of themselves in terms of external ideas about the reality of a situation or preconceived notions of how a life ought to be lived.

TWO

Writers and their problematic (perhaps self-serving) notions of the truth. The malleability of memory. Fixing memories versus raiding the memory-store to rewrite the life-story. The allure of self-invention. Social consequences of free self-invention.

The patient's truth in the therapeutic encounter. Dynamic (evolving) truth. The mediating role of the therapist. Intersubjective truth. Sympathy. The role of the heart, the role of the mind. Shared social experience as constraint on reckless self-invention. The lessons of art. The encounter with the artwork as an intersubjective experience. Learning to be free to inhabit one's own perspective; a clinical example.

JMC – I feel I must press further on the question I raised last time: Is the goal of the therapist (deliberately I don't write, the goal of therapy) to bring the patient face to face with the true story of their life or to provide them with a story of their life that will enable them to live more adequately (more happily, which in the minimal Freudian prescription amounts to being able to love and work again)? How flexible can therapy afford to be in actual practice? Of course the therapist always desires the ideal outcome, the whole truth and the embracing of the whole truth by the patient; but given the constraints of time and money, doesn't the therapist more often than not have to settle for a good-enough outcome, a truth that is not the whole truth but is good enough to get the patient back in working order?

When I read Freud in his less pessimistic moments, I do find him echoing, in what seems to me a rather unquestioning way, the prescription: You shall know the truth, and the truth shall set you free. My question is: If the goal of therapy is to set the patient free, is the truth the only avenue to freedom? Will a *version* of the truth, not as comprehensive as the whole truth, and perhaps tailored to the demands of the moment (the demands of the present juncture in the patient's life), not do equally well, if the goal is to get the patient back on the rails?

I find the question urgent because, since at least Plato's time, the accusation against poets (that is, people who make up stories) is that their allegiance is not first of all to the truth. Poets typically defend themselves by saying that they do believe in the truth, but that they have their own definition of what constitutes truth. When their definition is investigated, it usually turns out to be a mixed one. Poetic truth is in part a matter of reflecting the world accurately ('truthfully'), but also in part a matter of internal consistency, elegance, and so forth – in other words, a matter of satisfying autonomous aesthetic criteria.

The heart of Plato's case against the poets is that, when it comes to a choice between truth and beauty, they are too ready to sacrifice truth. The heart of the poets' case is that beauty is its own truth.

You will find some version of the beauty-is-truth plea in the practice of almost any writer. 'I may be making up this story, but for mysterious reasons that have to do with its internal coherence, its plausibility, its sense of rightness and inevitability, it is nevertheless in some sense true, or at least it tells us something true about our lives and the world we live in.'

The poet, says Plato, persuades us of the truth of his version of the way things are, and persuades us using the full armamentarium of poetic tricks and devices. The poet is thus like the rhetorician, whose goal is not to get to the truth but to swing you around to his way of thinking.

I return to the therapeutic situation. What prevents me, as therapist, from setting myself the goal of using what the patient tells me to come up with a persuasive (that is, plausible) narrative of what the patient's life has been, up to now, and a persuasive sketch of how that narrative line may be continued into the future in such a way that the patient may love and work productively in the world?

The obvious answer is: I am prevented by my allegiance to the truth. But in practice can the truth – the whole truth – be attained without interminable analysis? And if interminable analysis is not practical, why not settle for a version of the truth that, in some sense, works?

∞

AK – The short answer to your question is yes, of course one must content oneself with a version of the truth that works. But my experience is that more often than not the truth IS what works – I can't really go along with the opposition between practicality and truth set out in your account. For a start, by the time people come to the point of asking to see a psychotherapist, they have often exhausted all plausible and common-sense explanations of what is going on and tried all available forms of practical aid. There is a need for the psychotherapist to help the patient dig deeper and come to a way of understanding why they are so unhappy that has not been possible before, usually because something painful or difficult cannot be faced. When this happens, however imperfect or incomplete, it feels like truth. Not historical or scientific or philosophical truth, but emotional truth.

I would like to say something more about the nature of truth in psychotherapy, because I think it is upon this that the matter hinges. Let us think for a moment of the way one's version of one's parents, say of one's mother, changes over the life course, so that in a psychotherapeutic conversation one can distinguish between the view of one's mother one had as a baby and the view one had as a child, as an adolescent, as a young adult with or without one's own children, as a middle-aged adult, and so on. Now it seems to me that if one thinks of this as an example of the way in which life-narratives develop in therapy, it is not that some fixed and external truth exists and is gradually and painstakingly accessed – in this case with regards to the person of one's mother and who she really was and is. Or at least, if this is the case, this is not the business of therapy as I understand it. More, it is that therapist and patient work towards an understanding of the way in which an intimate, formative relationship is experienced in the mind of the patient, based upon the important matter of perspective: where the patient is situated in terms of their own development and needs, their temperament, the nature of the relationship and the external situation as it is experienced by them. For this reason the truth in psychotherapy is in its essence dynamic because it derives from the perspective of a living being whose external and internal characteristics change, even in small ways, over time.

If one thinks about how, for example, a patient idealises their mother in order to protect themselves from the full force of their disappointment in her, the key thing is to help the patient to explore the emotional logic of the situation and understand where it fits in their development, and how the resulting frame of mind obstructs forward movement. One might do this by in effect removing a distortion and revealing something that feels to the patient more real and more true in the external world. But as a psychotherapist one aims to operate by working to understand the internal world of the patient, taking away the need for distortion through an understanding of that need – rather than by too much presenting of external truth. (To my mind, the latter scenario comes dangerously near to the sort of criticism and invalidation of emotional experience which leads people to therapy in the first place.)

Truth in psychoanalytic psychotherapy is internal truth – the truth of what is in the heart and the mind of the patient, perceived – and if one is lucky – understood, through the heart and the mind of the psychotherapist. For just as one tries to remain mindful that the patient is a perceiving subject, who experiences the world in their own unique way, and help them to be more aware of themselves as such, the psychotherapist is also a perceiving and feeling subject in relation to the patient as object. And it is this, the way in which therapy mirrors all acts of knowledge and understanding involving a subject and an object, which allows for a properly sympathetic and emotionally attuned exploration of the patient's mode of meaning-making.

So the truth which psychotherapy is based upon, or at least my version of psychotherapy, is always dynamic, provisional and intersubjective. It is contained within the terms of a relationship, which aims to reflect upon internal experience to help the patient to live as fully as possible in the world. It is also based, I think, on a belief than we can only know and understand ourselves fully through others – through the way we experience others and ourselves in relation to others, and the way others experience us.

This is what I read your book *Summertime* to be about.

JMC — Behind what you say there so obviously lies a weight of clinical experience and of prolonged reflection on that experience that I feel embarrassed to offer to reply. I have no experience behind me, from either side of the clinical dialogue; the case I put (and I wonder whether it even constitutes a case) sounds to me abstract to the point of airy-fairyness. But I shall press on anyway, as best I can.

Let me start by posing a philosophical question. What is an event itself, as opposed to the event as we interpret it to or for ourselves, or as it is interpreted to or for us by others, particularly authoritative others? 'When I was eight my father hit me with a tennis racket,' says a subject. 'Not true,' says his father. 'I was swinging the racket and accidentally hit him.' What really happened? Specifically, is the boy's memory of the event true, or is the father's true? I call it a memory, but that is an oversimplification: it is a memory-trace which has been subjected to a certain interpretation. I might even go on to say that it is a memory-trace which has been subjected to an interpretation behind which lies a certain will to interpret (in the boy's case perhaps a will to give the event its darkest interpretation, in the father's case a will to give it a harmless interpretation). How are we to disentangle the memory component from the component of interpretation, leaving aside for the moment the will behind the interpretation? Is it possible — philosophically but also neurologically — to speak of a memory that is pristine, uncoloured by interpretation?

Just recently I read an article by Jonathan Franzen in which he says that, after submitting to one promotional interview after another for his new book, he felt he had to break free or else he would begin to believe in the life-narrative that he had been spouting in the interviews. I interpret him as saying, not that he had been telling untruths in the interviews, but that the repetitions of a single account of his own life were scouring so deep a trace that he would soon lose his freedom to interpret (remember) his life otherwise.

To think of a life-story as a compendium of memories which one is free to interpret in the present according to the demands (and desires) of the present seems to me characteristic of a writer's way of thinking. I would contrast this with the way many people see their life-story: as a history that is forever fixed ('you can't change the past'). The strange thing is how many of us want to fix our life-story, by repeating over and over, to ourselves and to others, one or other preferred interpretation of it.

You can hear trivial examples of fixing a piece of history any day of the week as you sit in the bus eavesdropping on conversations. 'I said to her . . . She said to me . . . I said to her . . .'

You write of the changing ways in which one may be able to see the past according to one's age or personal development; you use the word *perspective*. I don't think you and I are far apart here. The therapist who comes up against the 'ordinary' notion that one's past (more accurately, the story of one's past) is immutable must surely experience it as an obstacle.

As I have said before, what interests me in these fixed life-stories is not so much what finds its way into them as what gets left out.

Leaving things out is, I suppose, **repression**; and the theory seems to be that the bits that have been left out are still there somewhere in the dark recesses of memory. I know the human brain is huge, but is it really big enough to hold everything that has been left out? Doesn't what we leave out add up to everything in the universe minus our small part? We leave it out, we say, because it isn't relevant. What that means is that it isn't relevant to the present interpretation we prefer to give to our past.

All of which leads me back to your suggestion that psychotherapists might be able to learn from writers (in this case fiction writers) how to aim at, or at least be satisfied with, a life-narrative whose truth is poetic (a hard term to define – later you write of 'the truth of what is in the heart and the mind', which may or may not be the same thing) rather than pragmatic, conforming to the facts of the case.

I would agree and might even be persuaded to go further: to say that the therapist might aim to foster in the patient a freedom to be master of their own life-narrative; that the sense of freedom or mastery, and what can be achieved with it, may turn out to be more important than the story itself.

The question, however, is whether we really want to move in a society in which everyone around us feels empowered (a term I use cautiously) to 'be who they want to be' by acting (acting out) the personal myths (the 'poetic' truths) they have constructed for themselves. Do we trust the human imagination as an invariable force for good? Doesn't the human imagination, in ninety-nine cases out of a hundred, fall back on the most banal of stories, picked up out of the commercial repertoire?

Where one would go from here I am not sure. On the one hand I am alarmed by the prospect of a world in which people's notion of liberty includes the liberty to reconstruct their personal histories endlessly without fear of sanction (fear of the **reality principle**). On the other hand, if an individual who is deeply miserable can be cheered up by being encouraged to revise the story of their life, giving it a positive spin, who could possibly object?

In the first case the truth seems to me to matter, finally. We can't all simply be who we like to think we are. In the second case the truth seems to me to matter less. What is wrong with a harmless lie if it makes us feel better? (Example of such a lie: After we die we wake up in another, better world.)

Help me to get beyond this point.

౦౦

AK – I can certainly try!

If I extrapolate a bit, the psychological alternatives I hear in your account are: a relationship with external reality, which is invoked as inhuman in a literal way – pure and interpretation-free and therefore above and beyond us (we refer to this I think as a moral imperative with phrases like 'get real' and 'face up to reality'); and on the other hand, an alarming situation where awareness of a coordinated, shared reality is minimal, and people are cut off from each other because of their absorption in wish-fulfilling fantasy and the stories that are most convenient to tell about their lives.

What is missing is a sense of us as living beings in the world: in this description it is as if we either exist only in our minds or, in some sense, not at all. External and internal experience are in combat, not in relation.

The idea of pure, external reality – a place in which an event takes place and is an event in and of itself alone – is not something I can intuit in anything other than a way that seems forced and wholly abstract. I can only proceed on the basis of my own experience – what else is there? – from which it follows that experience is absolutely a matter of perspective, whether individual or shared. That it takes place within the minds of living beings, I mean. But if experience is located within the minds of living beings, living beings are in turn firmly located in our shared world – the world of rocks and trees and rivers and concrete and cars and other people. So what I am saying is not in any way a disavowal of shared experience, of what is referred to as reality or common sense, but more a fairly simple observation regarding the site of our knowing. It is a plea for groundedness in our existence as subjective beings in the world.

It is artists – singers, painters, writers – who have most inspired me with a sense of the subjective and intersubjective nature of experience; who speak to me of how we cannot help but be ourselves, if only we could find the confidence to realise it; and of how we cannot but be influenced by others, those who came before us and those who live alongside us, in ways we can only begin to know.

The art I love seems to say this to me: 'Look at what is going on around you – in all its richness and detail and colour, its beauty and its ugliness; don't stop looking and thinking about what you see; but also don't forget that it is you who are looking, that you have a position and a place from where you look – and so do other people. Inhabit that place fully.'

This latter invitation, the invitation to inhabit one's perspective – to understand and own it for all its difficulty and its complexity in as mindful a way as possible – seems to me central to the practice of twenty-first-century, postmodern psychoanalysis. The point here is that all of us have a perspective – which is not static of course, but changes and develops – and we can choose, in the stories we tell ourselves about our lives, to be more or less true to it. We cannot simply substitute one perspective for another in the self-determining way you describe; or if we do so, there are considerable costs.

I recall a man who suffered childhood trauma, in this case abandonment by a parent, and largely dealt with it by putting the unpalatable experience out of mind. At one level he knew what had happened to him, having fixed upon a story of his life that included the trauma and was coherent, if limited in depth and scope. But he continued to struggle with the trauma as an emotional experience, in terms of its full impact upon him and the extent to which it had affected him at different stages of his development. The abandonment had been too much for him to deal with as a child, and the way he found of rising above his experience seemed to work – to do the trick, as it were. It was later down the line that he found himself in the grip of the **repetition compulsion**, unconsciously and repeatedly trying to repair the internal psychic situation, but unable to do so. He looked everywhere for love and validation, but was unable to find what he was looking for because the feelings of abandonment and neglect from childhood could not be consciously admitted. In short, he did not really know what he was looking for. This is not freedom – the freedom to pick a preferred version of one's life from the trees, as it were – but the opposite.

The freedom offered by psychoanalysis is the help of a willing and experienced other to explore and develop one's own perspective without inhibition and constraint, as far as such a thing is possible. To me this feels like a real, if sometimes terrifying, freedom. But there is a paradox, which is that in embracing this freedom one discovers aspects of one's experience, of oneself, that one cannot escape – much as one would like to.

THREE

Is it true that memories — neurological traces of past experience — are immutable? Are we not free to replace memories that distress us with invented memories that make us feel good? If we object to people making up their past, are our objections not purely and simply ethical? Classical psychoanalysis and its claim that we cannot repress inconvenient memories at will. The example of evil deeds: must the perpetrator's efforts to wipe them from the record be doomed to failure? Does such a claim not rest on faith in the ultimate justness (justice) of the universe?

How memory is treated in psychological theory. Procedural memory versus episodic memory. The experience of giving shape to a memory. The predicaments of real-life patients seeking therapeutic help: difficulties in making their life-story coherent; a fragmented sense of self; inability to integrate emotion with memory. Psychoanalytic theory and its nuanced treatment of strategies of defence (splitting, projection, repression). Repression

in the service of the development of the psyche versus repression
that obstructs development.

❖

JMC – There is an aspect of the psychological theory of what I am calling memory-traces with which I am still struggling, an aspect that may turn out to be central to distinguishing real life from fictional life, real people from people in books.

In the matter of reality versus fantasy, I think you misinterpret me. The poles I was suggesting are not (a) an interpretation-free reality beyond our reach (what I would call the noumenal) and (b) a wilfully self-created reality that one might as well call fantasy. One pole is certainly fantasy; but the other is a sense of one's self as immutably fixed because the history out of which one grew (the memories that make up one's past) is immutable, beyond one's control.

What I still don't grasp, at an empirical psychological level, even at a neurological level, is why those memories should be immutable – why they should not be amenable to revision, to being given an alternative spin, even at an extreme to being wiped out and replaced by more desirable memories.

I do think my problem is as elementary as that: Why can't I install a new set of memories that suit me better than the old ones? Or, to rephrase the question: Even if I have to accept that trying to install a set of new memories – a new past – doesn't work in practice, why can it not work?

I ask this question with the example in mind of how adults continually entrench memories in children: 'Don't you remember how . . .' I am properly wary of using myself as an example, but let me nevertheless assert that I have no memories of the time before I was about four that were not reinforced, if not actually installed, either by my mother's words or via a snapshot interpreted for me by my mother. 'Don't you remember? That was your third birthday. That was when we were living in that ugly old house in Warrenton, where it got so hot and the mosquitoes buzzed all night.'

I have a scar on my right thigh. The scar is there, so something must have caused it. But my only memory of what happened was supplied by my mother, who told me of an accident that occurred in 1942 as a result of which I had to have three or four or five stitches. 'And you were very brave. You didn't cry.' So I became the kind of little boy who doesn't cry. An instance of how implanted memories can exert a force well into the future.

There must be a standard answer to my question about the resistance of memory to being erased or supplanted, because it is such an obvious question. Yet even without knowing what the standard answer will be, I can foresee that I am going to be resistant to it. My sense of the malleability of memory is simply too strong.

I haven't yet got to your main point, which has to do with command (e.g. the command to inhabit one's own perspective). I seem to detect a certain ethical force behind this command, though you do say that it can be justified on common-sense grounds: if you choose to inhabit some fantasy perspective, there will sooner or later be a real-world price to pay.

And I concede that many of the great novelists stand behind you in this respect. Emma Bovary tries to live out a fantasy life (tries to live like the heroine in one of the romances she devours as an adolescent), but the world won't allow it.

But what if one chooses to operate on a much less grand scale than Emma? What if one makes up a fantasy past that doesn't lead one into conflict with the world, just makes one's life sound more interesting, and thus perhaps makes one happier? Surely you cannot deny that there are people like that in real life, people who don't like the past they have been given and have replaced it with a better one?

I concede, I too tend to think of this way of operating as 'wrong'. In that respect I am of Flaubert's school. But I would be hard put to say why it is wrong.

So, as you can see, I am still stuck.

∞

AK – I share your sense of the malleability of memory. Indeed the more I think about it, the more malleability seems to me intrinsic to the process of remembering.

I ask myself, what is memory? What is it and what is it for? The term refers to a variety of forms of encoding or representing experience (there is verbal memory, visual and sensory memory, for example) for the purpose of learning and development across the lifespan. At a basic level we all need to remember in order to master the most basic behavioural repertoires, and we carry on using memory throughout life as a way of reflecting upon experience to learn from it. From this angle, the urge to fix the story of our lives may be an aspect of a largely adaptive drive to rehearse the lessons of the past, issuing implicit instructions to ourselves in the present.

The psychological literature identifies two main memory systems: procedural memory, which is non-verbal and enables the carrying-out of action sequences such as walking, climbing, driving, and so on; and episodic memory, which relates to the ability to code experience in verbal, and more specifically, narrative terms – the type of memory we rely on to tell ourselves and other people about what happened. Episodic memory is dependent on language and so isn't thought to exist before the age of about four, which entirely fits with your experience, whereas procedural memory operates from the beginning of life.

At the moment I write detailed notes of therapy sessions every week to take for discussion with a clinical supervisor, often four to five pages long. If I sit down to write immediately after a full session and before any processing has taken place it feels as if I can't remember anything because the raw material from the session is so formless. If I return to the write-up a few hours later my mind will of its own accord have started to impose a shape on the interactions, which makes it more possible to construct an account of the session. I am often aware of the inevitably selective attention I give to certain aspects of the experience that seem to me interesting or relevant to other thoughts about the case. Some aspects of the session are edited out, others are given particular emphasis or meaning in the way they are reported in the write-up. I can observe how hard it can be to remember a particular part of the session, or how confused I am about the order of things. I can also catch my mind playing tricks on me, creating its own semi-fictional sense of how things happened, influenced presumably by an underlying sense of plot or narrative in relation to the encounter.

It seems to me it is in such work, such small-scale mouldings and shapings of experience through representation, that memory occurs.

In relation to your concerns it is probably useful to think about such memory-shaping in terms of degree, the extent of the distortion of experience; emotional relevance, distinguishing for example between an account of an episode that leaves out an event of significance from one which edits out less important things, or which splits emotion off from memory; and also self-knowledge – the extent of the subject's awareness of these processes.

But the thought I come to is this: that when people seek psychotherapeutic help because they are in distress there is usually a real breakdown in the overall coherence of memory systems and the accompanying sense of self – the way the different parts fit together, if you like. In the consulting room we see people who communicate things about themselves, often unconsciously, which are at odds with the story they consciously tell. It is as if there is a discordance between early non-verbal memory, an aspect perhaps of procedural memory, and the episodic or story-telling memory system. A woman comes whose story is about how competent and capable she is, and she is clearly mystified by repeated failures in relationships. But in some way she seems as vulnerable and young (much younger than her years) and in intimate relationships she is so needy and demanding that she ends up driving people away. A man presents himself as much admired by women, talking proudly of his abilities as a seducer, but the only point at which he shows emotion is when he talks of his father, and he is clearly seeking close male friendship but not getting the intimacy he desires. And so on . . .

Of course all of us are at odds with ourselves and with others to a greater or lesser extent – but the sense of disconnectedness is extreme in these people, at least at the point they seek help. And the issue here really does seem to be one of fit rather than the accuracy of memory, at least for the purposes of understanding human suffering.

♋

JMC – Your account of what goes on while you write up your notes in the wake of a therapeutic session is fascinating. Has anyone paid attention yet to this phase of the relationship between patient and therapist – a phase from which the patient is wholly absent, and the therapist works alone to give a true rendering of what happened during their meeting, trying to exclude the interference (in a radio-wave sense) of forces from the therapist's own life?

I do believe I realise how abstract my scenarios are in comparison with the actual therapeutic situations you experience, where there is an immediately striking disjunction between the patient's words and the evidence offered not only by their history but also by the drama that their physical body plays out before your eyes. Nevertheless, let me press on.

What continues to trouble me is the notion of a self constructed on the basis of memories that one may wish to call false (fictional), except that their falsity is indeterminable because the 'real' history to which they appeal for support is irrecoverably lost in the past, and also because the person who has created this (perhaps) false past is happy with it and has no reason to subject themself to the eye of a professional doubter (a psychoanalyst, for example) whose business might be to undermine it.

Here we enter the classical theory of repression, with which I am familiar only through Freud, so if theory has moved on, please correct me.

The classical theory, as I understand it, asserts that repression cannot succeed: whatever is repressed here manifests itself there, though perhaps in so heavily disguised a form that only a trained specialist can track it back to its roots. (At the same time, Freud says, repression is necessary: repression is the basis of civilisation; it is what distinguishes human beings from the beasts.)

The claim that repression cannot succeed – and consequently that we are not free to create our own past – seems to me to rest finally on faith in the justice of the universe. What we gain in repressing what we do not want to remember we have to pay for via the subterranean poisoning of other aspects of our life.

But there seems to be all too much evidence that such faith is unfounded. To give an extreme example, certain people who have committed vile acts – torture, murder – seem able to construct life-stories (memories) for themselves out of selected fragments of the real (the long hours they had to work, the gratitude of their superiors, the promotions and medals they received) and to live with and by such memories, repressing all the ugliness.

Classical theory, at least in its popular version, says that such people have unhappy relations with their wives and children. It says they suffer from nightmares. It says that they are secretly haunted by the cries of their victims – by what they try and fail to repress of their 'real' past.

And indeed, if you put a torturer on trial or if you compel him to undergo a course of psychic rehabilitation, he may indeed begin to recollect those 'repressed' cries. If memory is malleable in the one direction, obliterating what disturbs the subject, it is surely malleable in the opposite direction too. If memories from which cries are absent are regarded dubiously, why should memories that include cries be any less dubious? The question is not whether somewhere there is a child who is crying; the question is whether the memory of the crying child is true and truly felt.

Which leads me to a quandary, as I think it should have led Freud. By the nature of things, the analyst does not often get to see happy people. The records of psychoanalysis are biased toward people for whom (in my account) repression has been tried but has not worked. It is not the rare, extreme case of the torturer that troubles me, but the much more frequent cases of people for whom repression – which at this point we can go back to calling forgetfulness – has worked, and has in fact become the foundation of a happy and successful life.

∞

AK – The principle at work in what you describe is not one of justice, since those who suffer trauma through no fault of their own can find themselves compelled to come to terms with the past just as those who deal it out. It is more, if raised to the status of an ethic, that of humility in the face of emotional and unconscious experience.

There is a crucial distinction to be made between repression that acts to protect the psyche and thereby serves a developmental cause, and repression that functions to obstruct development and is more defensive than protective in character. The former contributes to the foundation of a happy and successful life; the latter does not. Often, as I see it, it is only time that tells the difference between the two.

In my view classical theory does not present repression as doomed to failure, but as a highly successful way of protecting the psyche from discomfort and pain – a psychological corollary to natural anaesthetic in the biological realm. There is a common misconception that psychoanalysis represents psychic defences as inherently unhealthy and upholds the fantasy that we ought, if only we knew how, to live without defences. But in fact the psychoanalytic literature contains extensive descriptions of a range of defensive processes and systems, which are pretty much intrinsic to human experience. Each has its own developmental value in protecting the psyche at particular stages of vulnerability or need and in organising experience in certain ways. (In other words, there is no defence-free zone: just as we cannot escape subjectivity, we cannot get beyond the defences which delimit and protect perception and perspective.)

Problems come when defences are overused and misapplied. So **splitting**, dividing the world and the self that perceives that world according to separate qualities – good and bad, friendly and hostile, and so on – is an effective way of structuring perception from the earliest stages of life. It works well in pressured situations requiring action such as competitive sport or war. But it leads to problems if it dominates in intimate relationships. **Projection**, the business of locating oneself imaginatively in another person and identifying oneself with them, is the basis of all human sympathy. But it produces a sense of psychological impoverishment and no small measure of emotional confusion when a person projects in a way that is fixed and irreversible. Repression of libidinal feelings towards one's parents is a necessary part of adolescent development. It creates the space for a young person to separate from their family and form significant relationships in early adulthood. But problems ensue if the repression of loving feelings becomes an entrenched habit.

Does this take things forward?

FOUR

Oedipus Rex as a story whose moral is that the past cannot be buried. Why a story with the opposite moral seems not to be feasible. Dostoevsky's critique (in The Possessed) of claims to complete self-awareness. The Scarlet Letter *as the story of someone who accepts the consequences of her actions but privately denies the right of society to judge her. Comparable behaviour among real-life criminals.*

Real-life constraints on erasing our past. The Scarlet Letter *as an exemplary story about embracing, not erasing, a shameful past. Dostoevsky's Christian understanding of the motive for Raskolnikov's confession in* Crime and Punishment. *Freud's rereading of that motive. Distinguishing true from self-serving confession in clinical practice. Melanie Klein's thinking about guilt and reparation.*

❖

JMC – Let me explain why I say that the belief that we are not free to make up our own past must be based on faith in the justness of the universe.

One of the basic story-plots has the following shape. During his youth a man (it is usually a man) commits a shameful act, perhaps even a crime. He runs away, covers his tracks, takes a new name, makes a new life for himself in some faraway place. Years pass. He marries and has children; he becomes a pillar of the new community. He begins to allow himself to think his secret is safe, he has escaped his past. Then one day a stranger arrives in town and begins asking nosy questions. Implacably, step by step, the man's secret is uncovered. He is shamed; he is ruined. There are many novels built on such a plot (think of Thomas Hardy). The experience of reading them is interesting. Insofar as we identify with the hero, we do not want his secret to come out – we do not want the truth to emerge. In this respect such novels are the opposite of the detective novel, where we identify not with the man with the buried past but with the nosy intruder. (*Oedipus Rex* combines the two forms: Oedipus is both the owner of the buried past and the detective.)

I come to the point. The story is about the futility of trying to escape from one's past, of trying to reinvent oneself. The past (the past self) refuses to be buried.

In the story, read as an allegory of psychic processes, the self (the hero) never forgets his secret past – he is haunted by it – but he hopes he can keep it inside, bottled up. The hero's will thus stands for the agency within the psyche that seeks to repress uncomfortable, shameful memories, to keep them from consciousness. Consciousness itself is represented by society, by public awareness.

Novels that use this plot implicitly teach a lesson, as indeed do detective novels that use the plot's mirror version. The lesson is that we cannot escape from our past, that we are not free to reinvent ourselves. Such novels are often quite gripping: as we read them, the attempt – the doomed attempt – to preserve the secret gradually becomes our own attempt. Why so? Perhaps because each of us, in one way or another, cherishes the hope of remaking our own life, and is reluctant to concede that our past is inescapable.

Now imagine a story that tries to teach exactly the opposite moral: that our lives are ours to make and remake as we wish, that the past is past, that secrets can freely be buried and forgotten. Can there be such a story that works as a story? Can we have a story that ends, 'And his secret was forgotten and he lived happily ever after'?

Insofar as it ends in a paradox – the secret is not really buried, since the reader knows it – you cannot have such a story, at least not in its straightforward, unironic version. In other words, not only the moral-religious tradition in which we are brought up, but the tradition and perhaps even the very form of the story, refuse to concede that the past can be buried.

There is a sense in which the great plot-shapes submit to, or evoke, the notion of justice. That is to say, the story that can be told – the story of the man who tries but fails to bury the past – tells us something about cosmic justice; whereas the story that cannot be told – the story of the man who buries the past and lives happily ever after – cannot be told because it lacks justness.

But what if the true secret, the inadmissible secret, the secret about secrets, is that secrets can indeed be buried and we can indeed live happily ever after? What if this big secret is what the Oedipus-type story is trying to bury? In other words, what if our culture, perhaps even human culture in general, has created a form of narrative which is on the surface about the unburiability of secrets but under the surface seeks to bury the one secret it cannot countenance: that secrets can be buried, that the past can be obliterated, that justice does not reign?

As you see, the question of the secret, remembered or forgotten, continues to gnaw at me. I would like to believe that the universe is just, that there is some or other eye that sees all, that transgressions of the Law do not ultimately go unpunished. But a voice keeps asking: Is that really so? Is everyday life not bursting with examples of people who have forgotten what it is not convenient for them to remember, and prosper nonetheless?

It is against this background that I read what you say about repression (forgetting) as a mechanism that allows us to protect ourselves while we grow. What happens to justice, I ask myself, if we are free to ignore aspects of the past in the name of personal growth? At what point does the deployment of repression in the cause of personal fulfilment become culpable? While my parents are sleeping I smother my baby brother in his crib, and the coroner calls it apnoea, and I become king of the castle. Does the repressed memory of this act poison every day of my life until at last I confess it (submit to the Law) and do penance and am absolved;

or on the contrary can I successfully forget all about it and live a contented, blameless life?

Question one: committed by a three-year-old, is such an act culpable? Question two (the real question): Who is ever to find out about it if I, the sole witness of the act, have successfully repressed my own memory of it?

This is Dostoevskian territory. If there is no God, where is the sense in it all?

ം

AK – I'm pretty sure it's not right to go around hurting other people and then deal with it by putting the matter out of mind. Or to put it another way, if you are the kind of person that does this, sooner or later the world will cotton on and relationships with other people are going to be very difficult indeed. From the psychoanalytic point of view, it is not just a matter of it being wrong to behave in this way and justice needing to be done to achieve some measure of vindication. The more important point is that, because we are social beings, because we exist in relation to others and we need relationships with others, issues of personal well-being and social morality are deeply, inextricably related – they are not always the same but they are related.

I respond differently to the story of the-man-with-the-shameful-secret-turned-good. Why do we identify with such a figure? Why do we feel protective of him – of the life he has created for himself and of his secret? Partly I think it is because we sympathise with and we applaud the protagonist's urge towards reparation. We understand that it is not *despite* having committed a shameful act that he now puts such efforts into making good, but *because* of it; that the shameful past and the worthy present are connected, not separate, parts of the narrative, and some sort of reckoning, even of the most private kind, has taken place to get from one to the other. (Were the protagonist simply trying to escape from his past and not learning from it or facing up to it in any way, our identification would naturally fall in with the forces trying to uncover it.)

Let me retell the story of someone with a shameful secret, but in this case an open secret. The story is Hester Prynne's in Hawthorne's *The Scarlet Letter*. Hester lives in a Puritan settler-community in seventeenth-century North America. While waiting for her husband to join her she becomes pregnant by another man, and when the community finds out about her pregnancy she is required to wear a red letter A standing for adulteress as a mark of her disgrace. Hester sews ribbons and all manner of pretty things onto her scarlet letter; she embroiders it and decorates it, turning it into something to which she is in the end too attached to remove when told she can do so. She turns the mark of her disgrace into something else, part acceptance of what she has done, part defiance of the social reaction to this act (for the decoration goes against the Puritan dress code). But she transforms it into something that is creatively her own.

The Scarlet Letter tells us implicitly about trying to accept shameful vulnerabilities and mistakes – not just as individuals but as a community. It also speaks, I think, about the possibility of freedom for self-invention in the face of adversity – or I should say, out of adversity. For Hester's loveability as a heroine arises from the fact that she both embraces and defies her censure, managing not to sidestep what she has done and the meaning of this for others, but to make out of it her own story.

Freud read Dostoevsky, of course. It is hard to imagine Freud constructing the concept of the **superego** without having encountered Dostoevsky's study of a man who, compelled to act in his own defiantly anti-religious terms, kills an elderly female pawnbroker, and afterwards finds that he is, despite himself, completely taken over by remorse. There is something inside Raskolnikov that will not let him simply dispose of Christian ideas of right and wrong, that registers his transgression in a part of him that is outside conscious control. If you are Dostoevsky, or a Dostoevskian, you take the story to be about a part deep inside us (the soul) that is in accord with a higher purpose, that needs such a purpose and, through the force of that need, brings into being a spiritual reality. If you are Freud, or a Freudian, the story is likely to be read as being about the force of internal prohibition that was later described in his theory of the superego.

From the point of view of our discussion, however, the story that emerges – via Dostoevsky, Freud, Klein and many others – is one of humans as intrinsically social animals, that is to say, beings to whom relationships with others are fundamentally significant. To the Dostoevskian, this significance is of a sacred nature, while to the psychoanalyst relationships with others are a crucial aspect of selfhood.

∞

JMC – Remorseful confession has a long and complicated history in its literary embodiments. The part of this history that interests me – and has been of use to me as a writer – commences in England of the late seventeenth century, when journalists appropriated the confessions of criminals due to be executed for sensational material, and reaches a high point in the novels of Dostoevsky, who was no stranger to sensationalism but who was – I agree with you – unexcelled in the power of his diagnosis of the complex motives that may underlie a decision – or an impulse – to bare one's heart. Anyone involved in the therapeutic process ought to read Dostoevsky closely.

There is no single text that gives one the full range of Dostoevsky's treatment of confession and its motives. One needs to look not only at *Crime and Punishment*, but also at *Notes from Underground*, *The Idiot* and *The Possessed*. I don't want this to turn into a long discourse on Dostoevsky, so let me simply take up *The Possessed*, in particular the famous suppressed chapter – suppressed because Dostoevsky's publisher thought it would lead to a ban on the book by the censor.

In this chapter a landowner named Stavrogin tells a priest, Tikhon, about a particularly odious act he has committed:

seducing and debauching a twelve-year-old girl, then sitting idly by while she hangs herself. Tikhon's response is quite brusque. He asks why Stavrogin is making this confession to him, and suggests that his ultimate motive may be to be admired, if abhorred, as a Great Criminal.

The figure of the Great Criminal – built on the model of the self-made Napoleonic Great Man – interested Dostoevsky deeply as a phenomenon of the age. Raskolnikov, in *Crime and Punishment*, explicitly models himself on Napoleon. In effect the perverse new Great Man issues a challenge to God: I reject your commandments, what are you going to do about it? Stavrogin is a more self-conscious version of Raskolnikov. What does it say about your God, he says to Tikhon, that he can allow me to do what I have done? As Stavrogin would like to see it, the crime he has committed is no ordinary crime, but a philosophical crime committed in a philosophical spirit, a crime in which the victim, the child, is really only a pawn.

This claim on Stavrogin's part – that the nature of a crime is transformed if the perpetrator is rationally aware of what he is doing and why he is doing it, and that his own confession is no ordinary confession by a sinner to a priest, since it can be situated as part of a project of challenging God (or challenging the claim that the universe is good) – is rejected by Tikhon. To Tikhon, Stavrogin's claim to total self-consciousness – understanding why he committed the crime, understanding why he is confessing to it, understanding why he is laying bare his understanding of why he is confessing, and so forth in infinite regression – is only an elaborate smokescreen, behind which lies the banal ambition of an idle young man to become a celebrity by the shortest means available.

Tikhon's position in the exchange is not exactly that of a therapeutic counsellor (though one might argue that what Stavrogin needs most of all is the shock treatment of being seen through). He is better thought of as a detective, in the same line as Porfiry Petrovich in *Crime and Punishment*. Within his dialogue with Stavrogin – which is better thought of as a duel – the respective positions are (Stavrogin's) that if one's intellect is clear and dispassionate enough, total self-knowledge is possible; and (Tikhon's) that what presents itself as self-knowledge may well be a self-serving obfuscation of what is often likely to be the simple truth.

The figure who interests me in the duel is Tikhon, as the one who is placed in the position of being confessed to by the one who wants to – or claims to want to – make confession. In *Notes from Underground*, and in the many novels and stories in European literature that follow after *Notes from Underground*, it is the reader who is manoeuvred into the Tikhon position, and has to decide whether what they are reading is a 'true' confession or (for instance) a pseudo-confession whose unstated purpose is to make one think more highly of the narrator. In the twentieth century, decoding the motives behind speech-acts becomes one of the main constituents of a literary education, and one of its main claims to social relevance. Reading a novel by Henry James in school time is justified as a training in how to survive in a world where what people say is not always what they mean.

I am not sure that the Stavrogin-like position can always be brushed aside as summarily as Tikhon does. Translated into a therapeutic context, I take Stavrogin to be saying that complete, lucid self-understanding is possible, even if such self-understanding does not tell one what to do about one's situation. Similarly translated, I take Tikhon to be saying that layer upon layer of (claimed) self-awareness is more than likely to be nothing more than a defence. Stavrogin implies that the conversation can go on for ever, because there is always a further level of self-understanding to be explored; Tikhon rejects this position and asserts his claim to the last word: the end of talk, the beginning of the work of repentance and reparation.

Let me now turn to Hester Prynne, who in every sense antedates Stavrogin (*The Possessed* was published in 1873, *The Scarlet Letter* in 1850). The action of *The Scarlet Letter* pivots on a long-delayed public confession, namely the confession of the young clergyman Arthur Dimmesdale that he is the father of Hester's child. Up to that point it is Hester who has alone borne the punishment pronounced by the Puritan elders: to be branded an adulteress and live on the fringes of society. Hester never acknowledges any criminal act, never confesses. She holds her silence throughout.

Hawthorne is a notably chaste writer, so if one wants to divine his attitude toward Hester's extramarital liaison one has to read a great deal into the one or two private moments when Hester takes off her Puritan cap and frees her rich and beautiful head of hair. These moments make Hester an unusually powerful sexual presence by Hawthornian standards, much more so than pale Dimmesdale (Hester is of course a woman of experience by the time of their liaison, whereas Dimmesdale, one suspects, is a novice).

Whatever the character named Hester is reported as thinking about her transgression, what Hawthorne seems to say in his physical presentation of her is that a society that oppresses such a woman has something wrong with it. Hester herself may not openly demand, 'What was my crime?' but Hawthorne's novel certainly seems to be asking so.

If we read the novel in this way, we cannot but reject the verdict society has pronounced on Hester. The Hester of our reading does not accept the story of her life that is foisted on her by the magistrates who wield power in the settlement, a story encapsulated in the letter A. She has a different story, which she keeps buried in her breast. This makes her a continual ironist: what she outwardly seems to be confessing to, via the scarlet letter she displays, is Adultery. But the letter is cryptic: what it may really stand for is 'Able' (the narrator's playful conjecture), or perhaps even some comment on her judges so searing that it cannot be written.

I see Hester as bowing to her punishment (the alternative to which would have been banishment from the settlement) while privately rejecting the judgment on her. In other words, I see Hester's unexpressed attitude toward the proscription of sexual activity on her part as very much that of a freethinking American woman of the 1840s, the kind of woman Hawthorne met on Brook Farm: *We may be powerless to resist, but we do not accept the moral basis of male power over us.*

Prisons are full of people who, in one important respect, are like Hester: they seem to accept their punishment and behave in every way like model prisoners well on their way to rehabilitation, but in fact they are secret ironists who reject the legitimacy of the law under which they were sentenced and the judges who pronounced sentence. To themselves and their closest friends, they say, 'Who gets to write the laws and administer them is a matter of power, not of justice. By their standards I am a criminal; by my standards I was just taking what was due to me (or exercising my rights as a free person).'

Refusing to acknowledge, inwardly, their guilt, and seeing themselves, privately, as victims of injustice, gives such people a powerful sense of righteousness. What they have done is precisely to take control of their life-story, even if to a Tikhon-like outsider the story they are telling themselves may look like a self-serving lie.

I don't see that such people, who may be lying to themselves but whose lies undoubtedly serve to empower them, giving them a sense of direction and control over their lives, are different in nature from the killers and torturers I discussed earlier, people who have some kind of story to tell themselves (patriotism, necessity, the fight against evil) that justifies all their actions.

(That, incidentally, is why I find the nostrum that each of us has a life-story, and we should exert ourselves to become the author of that life-story, rather than allowing others to tell it to or for us, to be morally dubious. The story that the Puritan magistrates attribute to Hester Prynne – foul deeds by night – is not necessarily the true story; and the story that Hester – the Brook Farm Hester – tells herself is not necessarily the true story – 'I did it for passion.' But both (a) the idea that we are free to choose between these two stories as we see fit, or make up another one, since there is no such thing as truth, just truth-for-you and truth-for-me; and (b) the idea that Hester's story must be a good story simply because it is Hester's, strike me as highly questionable.)

∽

AK – How interesting! And Dostoevsky's scepticism towards the truth-telling urge could hardly be more relevant today when magazines are full to bursting with the tales of soul-baring celebrities. They compete as to who can tell what is presented as the truest, the most private, the most authentically and deeply personal (and often the most sensational) story; and the reader is invited to take up the role of privileged confidant to the rich and famous.

What can we take from your reading of Dostoevsky into the therapeutic situation? There are probably many things, but for one we can take the observation that a person can have all the insight in the world but choose not to act upon it. Or further, as Tikhon suspects of Stavrogin, that insight can be used (or abused) to mask the fact that this is what is happening – to pull the proverbial wool over the therapist or therapist-confessor's eyes and ears. I have certainly come across patients whose apparent self-awareness is very misleading in this way – to themselves as much as to those around them.

But what I am interested in is what underlies or brings about true repentance or a true reckoning with oneself, rather than the sham or cynical variety, since it is the job of the therapist to tell one from the other and to work to promote genuine understanding over the pretend version, and if possible, the state of mind where such understanding can be put to use.

There is a wonderful moment after Tikhon has read Stavrogin's confession when Stavrogin asks for Tikhon's forgiveness, and Tikhon responds by making this conditional on Stavrogin's forgiveness of him. What Tikhon does at this point – and one cannot help but feel that Dostoevsky is speaking through him – is to illuminate the connection between Stavrogin's relentlessly psychopathic behaviour and his view of relationships, which is one which leads him to judge others as suspiciously and harshly as he imagines himself to be judged. In this state of mind Stavrogin is only capable of hatred and self-hatred, and his self-flagellation is an integral part of the problem rather than any sort of solution or resolution to it.

Klein's ideas about the development of guilt and the urge

towards reparation come to mind. A brief description of her formulation of the paranoid-schizoid and depressive positions will first be necessary.[1]

The paranoid-schizoid position dominates in the first months of life and is a primary state of mind for all of us. In it other people are experienced as parts and not three-dimensional wholes. Psychic defences are brought into force in response to a strong sense of external threat. Splitting and projection are used to get rid of ambivalent feelings: things in the world – people and objects – are ordered in relatively simple, black-and-white terms and negative feelings are disowned by locating them in other people.

This means that a sort of primitive superego is often in operation, which results from the projection of frustration and hatred. These feelings are dealt with by putting them into the Other, rather than thinking about them as an aspect of the self, and this Other then becomes increasingly alien and threatening and is taken in and represented inside the mind in this way. This is the state of mind that produces monsters and bogeymen, and the paranoid person is someone who comes to live their life under the sway of such persecutory figures.

In good circumstances movement towards the depressive position starts to take place in the second part of the first year of life. This state of mind is characterised by the internal representation of significant others as three-dimensional and whole, and as made up of different parts, some of which give rise to feelings of frustration and hatred, and others to feelings of satisfaction and love. The world can no longer be divided up in straightforward terms, and the complex, mixed feelings evoked in relationships are experienced as originating from inside the self instead of having to be defensively got rid of by locating them in external objects.

Guilt and the capacity for concern and reparation are born out of the realisation that the person whom we can feel we want to cast aside, even momentarily, because they frustrate or disappoint us is the very same person we love and depend upon. They result from awareness of this internal conflict, in which the capacities for creativity and destructiveness in each of us are acknowledged simultaneously and at a feeling level. They are not, to use Tikhon's phrase, just *ideas* of guilt and remorse that come from outside in the form of obligation or duty, but have real, internal meaning.

(If we shift our focus to the individual's relationship with society, guilt and the reparative urge are dependent upon an awareness of one's attachment to the community, even if it is a highly ambivalent attachment, and the extent to which the community provides basic help and succour – a livelihood, a sense of identity, and so on.)

It is not as if this type of thinking is something one masters, once and for all; oscillation between the two positions is an integral part of life and, for most of us, a more paranoid and fragmented state of mind can take hold when we are stretched or unwell. The main point here, however, is that real concern and remorse – rather than the idea of them – are a genuine developmental achievement, not something that can be produced to order.

As I see it, there is an apparent paradox, which is that traditional forms of punishment, which have remorse as one of their aims, tend instead to result in internal rebellion and relief from guilt. The offender may be behind bars, giving some measure of satisfaction to society's desire for vengeance. But in the face of social exclusion and rejection the offender is more likely, in the privacy of their own mind, to harbour the sense that they have been treated unjustly and are in the right – to, as it were, free themselves from responsibility at an internal level. A robust therapeutic response, one which can face up to what the **patient-offender** has done but think in a compassionate and meaningful way about it, has more chance of producing real remorse, rather than the idea of remorse.

FIVE

Dialogue between two human beings as interactions between projected fictions. The Turing Test for true human dialogue. Sympathy as a faculty of projecting oneself into the experience of the other. Can the faculty be acquired? Writing and reading as claimed instances of dialogue; scepticism about such claims. Dialogue and prayer. A terminological issue: 'entering into therapy' versus finding someone to talk to. Sacramental versus secular confession. Romantic myths of the artist as spiritual diagnostician.

Neville Symington on the relationship between patient and therapist: the moment of fusion and the moment of separation as stages in the growth in the patient's self-knowledge. Catholic confession versus Protestant self-scrutiny in the genealogy of psychotherapy. The resolutely secular, anti-magical ethic of psychotherapy. The patient's fundamental need to find a container for their experience. The therapist's task: to show the patient how experience can be thought about (given form), then to give the experience back.

❖

JMC – The passage you mention, where Tikhon asks Stavrogin to forgive him, reflects what I see as Dostoevsky's fundamental moral position regarding true interchanges between human beings (human souls), namely that these have to be reciprocal. Only when there is reciprocity do we have true dialogue.

From what I have written earlier – that I believe most exchanges between human beings to be exchanges between projected fictions – you may conclude that I am disqualified from, or at least unsuited to, judging between true and fake dialogue. I will certainly concede that my acquaintance with true dialogue is slight. In this respect I feel that I represent the norm; but you may think otherwise.

The so-called Turing Test for dialogue has always intrigued me: facing an interlocutor hidden behind a screen (or inside a computer), how can one be sure that the interlocutor is another human being and not an algorithm that picks up cues in one's speech and replies with preprogrammed sentences that sound like responses from another human being, that is, like answering dialogue?

Paradoxically, the Turing Test comes into its own in some of the more intense, indeed agonising scripts that every counsellor must be familiar with – for instance, the script that commences Everything I Do Is Meaningless, Why Should I Go On? Thus:

A. Everything I do is meaningless, why should I go on?

B. What do you mean, everything you do is meaningless?

A. I mean, my husband doesn't acknowledge the work I do in the house, the children don't speak to me, I don't get anything from my job. What is the point of it all?

B. Tell me about relations with your husband.

A. My husband comes home in a bad mood, he never asks what kind of day I have had.

B. What kind of day have you usually had?

It is the professional fate of the therapist to find herself at unpredictable moments trapped in pre-scripted exchanges like these. To catch oneself slipping into such an uncreative, mechanical way of talking, like a Turing machine, must be disturbing. But perhaps it is not just therapists who suffer such moments. Perhaps it is a risk all of us run when we don't have as much of an existential stake in the situation as our interlocutor does. Medical doctors must face the experience every day.

What does it require to enter into true dialogue? To begin with, it seems to me, two persons are required (two minds, two souls). Even the most gifted writer of dialogue cannot script a true dialogue between a human being and a machine. In the case of therapy – I make a bit of a leap here – this means that the therapist cannot be in true dialogue with someone who, willingly or unwillingly, remains caught in a round of mechanical complaints or accusations – who in effect remains the automatised half of the dyad. So part of the therapeutic trade must be skill in coaxing patients out of such fixed routines.

Yet at a deeper level dialogue requires a power of projecting oneself, via a faculty of sympathy, into the life-view and ultimately the being of the other. This projection of oneself cannot be into some imagined version of the other: it has to be into the actual being of the other, no matter how difficult and unpleasant and even boring that may be.

This power seems to me more than simply a professional one – a power that can be learned and passed on from one generation of the caste of healers to the next. In essence it seems to me spiritual.

In our earlier exchanges I think I failed to recognise that for true spiritual progress (let me use this term for the time being) to take place, true dialogue may be indispensable. The sort of self-created and self-creating narrative I wrote about, within which one insulates oneself from what to an outside observer looks overwhelmingly like the truth about oneself, is hard to break out of in isolation: the abstract imperative to face up to the truth is simply too painful to implement. One has to be helped; and no machine – no routine therapeutic patter that might as well be the output of a machine – can do the helping.

Thus, by a back route, I come to the case of the writer. Any analogy between writer and therapist, between the composition of fictions and the coaxing of patients into constructive ways of telling their life-stories to themselves, breaks down at this point. In the therapeutic situation there must be two persons, whereas stories are written (dictated) by one person. The difference is as simple as that.

I am rowing against a certain tide here, and I am aware of that. Let me note two currents in the tide. The first is the claim (by certain critics) that there is such a thing as the dialogical novel. The second is the claim (by many writers) that writing, at its most intense moments, is a matter of being dictated to rather than of dictating – that there have to be two persons or two souls in the room for a poem (in the widest sense) to get composed.

I won't discuss these claims in detail – not right now. But, as you can see, my scepticism about reading as a form of therapy remains unabated. (Writing as a form of self-therapy is a different matter – different but also smaller and less interesting.)

I am not unaware that the distance may not be great between 'true' dialogue and prayer. Prayer seems to me a neglected topic in contemporary therapeutic discourse – prayer and the prayerful state of mind. Am I wrong?

⁊⁊

AK – It's important not to idealise therapy and the therapeutic dialogue – something I need reminding of as much as you! The kind of true, growth-promoting dialogue of which you write is, I believe, difficult for any of us to achieve, and is more of an aspiration than anything else.

I'd like to open our own conversation up to consider the whole experience of a growth-promoting relationship, and not just dialogue – which to my mind belongs in the intellectual rather than the affective realm.

I read an interesting paper by the psychoanalyst Neville Symington about what he calls the 'moment of freedom' in the therapeutic relationship.[2] I took what he said as relevant to any relationship in which there is a strong bond, and in which the fostering of development is an aim. Symington writes about two stages, or moments, of relationship. The first is a moment of fusion when what is important is to go along with the needs, indeed with the illusions, of the other. To, in short, give them what they want – within reason, of course. It produces a particular sort of knowledge, a feeling type of knowledge rather than the intellectual sort, of another person because it allows a relatively free response at the unconscious level. But in an objective sense it allows us to say very little about the other person, since we have, to an extent at least, lost ourselves in someone else.

Later – for in his scheme it is later – he describes a different moment when one gives oneself permission to metaphorically step back and take possession of one's own mind and view the other in a way that is colder, keener, and altogether more separate. This moment is one of separateness, a moment in which there are two distinct people and an edge between them. It produces another type of knowledge, which is particularly necessary for development and which builds upon the knowledge gained by the moment of fusion. And in Symington's scheme it is at this later moment when one sometimes has to allow oneself to think the unthinkable, at least according to the previous terms by which the relationship has been lived. I should add that the unthinkable doesn't necessarily refer to anything radical or dramatic or scary, so much as the possibility of understanding from an unfamiliar vantage point, which allows one to see and feel things newly and differently.

Anyway, I think that the two types of relationship both have their place in the business of knowing another person and of knowing oneself in relation to another person, and that they produce different types of knowledge, neither of which is complete.

Last but by no means least, I would like to turn to the question of why you refer to spiritual development and to the prayerful state of mind. I ask you to expand upon this because although I am not religious these terms are meaningful to me. And the shift from the material to the spiritual register – the question of why and how this shift feels necessary or compelling – interests me very much.

∞

JMC – I will get on to the prayerful state of mind in due course. But first I want to pick out a few of the terms you have been employing and explain why I don't use them myself. For it would be unfortunate if we were to discover, somewhere down the road, that we have understood important words differently.

To begin with, I am reluctant to use the word *growth* in the same way that you do because I don't think we enter into therapy (or make confession, as I suggest later) with so abstract a goal in mind. In fact I wonder whether 'entering into therapy' itself is a good way of talking about what people do in real life. What happens, it seems to me, is that we feel a more or less pressing need to talk to someone, but not just anyone – someone who is 'right'. We may by this time have discussed our woes with a range of people, may even have worn some of them down – or worn them out – with our talk. But these people have turned out not to be 'right' for our purposes: our exchanges with them have been unsatisfying, have not given us what we feel in need of.

So instead of 'entering into therapy' I want to fall back on the vaguer idea of seeking the right person to talk to; and instead of 'wanting to grow' as a goal, I prefer to hold to a more primitive and unarticulated or inarticulate and unarticulable feeling of need – in this case a need to talk.

Then there is the term *communicate* itself. My understanding of communication is a fairly technical one. For an act of communication to take place, a number of requirements have to be met. Among these are: two participants, an I and a You, prepared to both emit and receive messages; and a shared code.

In the kind of life-situation you and I (a different you-and-I pair!) are concerned with, these requirements are met only in a highly problematic way. I am in doubt to or about myself (Am I one or am I fragments precariously held together by what I fear may be a fiction?); You are in doubt in various ways (Are You the right one? Do You really hear me or are You 'dead' to me?); and the code may be the very heart of what is wrong (When I say X, do You understand X or Y? To what social role do I submit when I accept the use of this code?).

Instead of communicating, then, I would stay with a more primitive notion of speaking – speaking by itself, not even speaking-to – with the reservation that at times speaking may turn into something more primitive, like tears: I am looking for someone before whom I can cry, or, in a metaphor that might cover both words and tears, before whom I can pour myself out.

I find myself more in tune with your account of what is required in the figure of You, the figure of the therapist, namely a not easily explained capacity for experiencing the other (the one I call I, or in this context Person 1) from the inside, the ability (the wisdom) not to be drawn into games, the study and experience and thought that enables You to understand, in at least one sense of this rich and complex word, what is going on in the other.

Now I broach a paradox: dialogue that may take the form of monologue.

I have been struck by how odd it is that there is not more reflection – at least that I am aware of – on the similarity between the therapeutic session and confession, as the latter works or is meant to work in the Catholic Church. Even odder when one notes that secular therapy had its growth spurt at just the time when the credibility of the claim by the Church to have the power and the right to forgive transgressions was waning.

The idea of confession that I want to work with is not the stereotypical one: Person 2 listening impassively, perhaps even half asleep, while Person 1 gabbles a list of 'sins', then imposing some routine penance or other before ritually absolving them. The formal elements I want to retain are: the silence (non-intervention) of the confessor (Person 2) during confession; the code of confession (the presumptively shared language); and the liberating formula with which the session ends.

Of course it is laughable that a five-minute confession can lift a lifetime's burden from our shoulders – laughable unless there is belief in its efficacy, shared by the two participants, at an intensity we can probably no longer imagine. (If Person 1 leaves the confessional in a state of rapture, as if walking on air, to all intents and purposes 'cured', we today would probably claim that the cure is illusory and that the burden will soon reimpose itself.)

But I wonder whether the whole massive body of analytic theory is not our secular (that is to say, disillusioned) substitute for the intense belief, shared between penitent and confessor, in the efficacy of the sacrament. The priest does not need to 'know' anything to bring about cure. He certainly has to understand, in the sense of reaching out sympathetically to the penitent, soul to soul. But for the rest it is the sacrament itself – what we might call the process – that achieves the cure.

The question that remains open, to my mind, is whether miraculous dialogue of this kind is lost for ever. (I call it dialogue because there are indeed two participants, the penitent on the one hand and the Holy Spirit on the other, speaking through the confessor.)

My inclination would be to say that it is not, or at least to hope that it is not.

There remains the question, however, of the code. Routine confession relies on a well-worn catalogue of sins, each with a standard name: false witness, fornication, taking the name of the Lord in vain, and so forth. We think to ourselves: How absurd that such a list – indeed, any standard-issue list – could throw light on our obscure sense that there is something wrong with us! We might also think: If I already know what 'is' wrong, if what 'is' wrong is what I have 'done' wrong, and I already know the word for that, then the problem is nine-tenths solved before I even enter the confessional.

In our experience, as post-religious people, Person 1 feels there is something wrong but has no idea what it is and certainly doesn't have a neat term for it; or else has a false idea.

Which brings us to the one who, at least in post-religious orthodoxy, is supposed to have the power to find the words for what is wrong, or what has gone wrong, or what we have done wrong, namely the artist, successor to the priest. While we sleep, the artist is awake. One of the master myths of Romanticism is of the artist and their wound. The wound is what keeps the artist awake, restless, in pain; the art that they produce may simply be intended to cure the wound (as the oyster tries to relieve the itch of the grain of sand by coating it in nacre), but it turns out to have wider uses. Along with the scientist-therapist, that other explorer of the dark world of the interior, the artist-priest has played the role of diagnostician of what is wrong with us; or at least played that role as long as the myth of the wound had currency.

For my part, I find too much self-aggrandisement in the idea – conjured up by artists themselves – of the artist as diagnostician of the age. There are further claims too, made of or by the artist, that I would take with a pinch of salt. One is that without the artist we ordinary folk would not have a language in which to talk about what is wrong with us. Another is that the artist as storyteller provides us with a model of how, by telling our story, we can empower ourselves and/or liberate ourselves from the grip of the past.

My inclination is to regard the stories that artists tell about themselves as much like the stories the rest of us tell about ourselves: they serve our own interests, or what we imagine are our interests. About every story we can legitimately ask: *cui bono?* Thus I come back to a theme I sounded at the beginning of our exchanges: that we should see the therapeutic dialogue as a quest for the truth before we see it as a way of making people feel good about themselves.

∞

AK – It is interesting that you associate the therapeutic dialogue with the Catholic ritual of confession – interesting because I see a link between Protestantism and therapeutic notions of individual responsibility, self-improvement and work on the self. To draw this line out, I would say that the psychotherapeutic project is both more modest and more ambitious than Catholic ritual: more modest because of its emphasis on the need to work hard and bear pain to produce even small results; more ambitious because of its location of the main site of meaning and transformation, not in God, but in the human self.

From what I understand as an agnostic non-Christian, in the confessional ritual the belief in the priest as a miracle worker, as the embodiment of God, is without question. He is given the power of absolution and invested with all the divine love and unconditional acceptance of the Holy Spirit. And it is thereby, in the terms of your metaphor, that the outpourings of sin, shame and suffering are removed, wiped away as tears by the loving parents of a small child.

Most psychotherapists strongly resist thinking of themselves as miracle workers, recognising the fantasy of providing a miracle solution as more of a trap than anything else. Patients commonly express a longing for cure or the waving of a magic wand, and the longing to provide it in return can be a powerful one. For many therapy could be said to start with the relinquishment of this longing, creating a space to think in a grounded and more modest way about problems and what it is possible to do about them. An apparent paradox then: real transformation in psycho-therapy hinges in part on the relinquishment of the desire for a miracle cure, and an acceptance of aims altogether more humble and more workaday.

It is not just a matter, in psychoanalytic psychotherapy, of the patient giving up magical thinking. This would be to greatly underestimate the hold magical thinking has on all of us. To begin with, the patient's sense of miraculous powers for good or ill, expressed in the form of exaggerated expectations of themself or an Other (often the therapist), is explored and given a free rein. But much of the work that follows is devoted to helping the patient take this power back into themself in a non-magical way. The aim is to undo a process of impoverishment of the self, whereby miraculous powers, such as fantasies of omnipotence or of an idealised Other, have been invoked by the unconscious mind as solutions to an underlying sense of weakness or insignificance. These feelings of misery and smallness in the patient, of the very opposite of the miraculous, are what need to be faced up to and understood in psychotherapeutic work – not to rub salt into the wound, but to help the patient move beyond them.

The better psychotherapists create conditions in which the most ancient of spells, of enchantment or bewitchment, are experienced at full strength – in order, eventually, to be broken.

I agree with you about the term *growth*: people don't generally seek out psychotherapy in order to grow or develop, aims which may mean a great deal to psychotherapists but seem abstract and irrelevant in the face of any immediate experience of unhappiness. But people do come to therapy desperately wanting to get unstuck or to move beyond a circle of thoughts going round in their heads, with no promise of release, no way of escape in which they can believe. In this sense they do not just want to talk; they want to be taken beyond their talk.

Like you I think we are looking, from the beginning of life, for a place to pour out what is inside us. But I think there is always truth, even of a distorted or an indirect kind, in any outpouring. How can there not be? What is inside is poured out, and the form it comes out in is usually not a matter of very much choice or conscious intent; it always involves distortions, whether big or small, which communicate something true, if only a listener can understand something of their relationship to truth (the principle of the distortion) and what lies beneath.

The stories we tell about our lives may not be an accurate reflection of what really happened, indeed they may be more remarkable for their inaccuracies than anything else. (I don't want to call them lies, although of course people do sometimes lie out of cynicism or shame.) But they are simply all we have to work with, or all that we know we have; and we can do a great deal with these stories, particularly if we take the view that there are truths, of the subjective and intersubjective kind, to be revealed in the manner of telling.

It is not just a matter of patients seeking an outpouring; psychotherapy is about more than simple evacuation – or if it isn't it certainly should be. What patients are looking for is a means of containing experience, in the sense of giving it form and meaning. The notion of containment is useful in describing how active the therapeutic process can be, while appearing fairly non-interventionist. It incorporates your account of the primitive need to pour oneself out, but moves beyond it in important ways.

It is not that any old form and meaning will suffice to provide containment of the helpful, therapeutic kind: the significance given to troubling and confusing experience, often unconscious, should be underpinned both by deep sympathy with the patient and a respect for emotional truth – however messy, complex or painful. So although the therapist needs to be sympathetic, he or she should also help the patient face up to things – and sometimes this is challenging and strenuous work. The two processes, the patient pouring out what is inside them and therapist and patient working together to give outpourings a form and meaning which is broadly sympathetic but also involves facing up to complex and painful truths, are interdependent. Patients are more able to talk freely if they find themselves in the company of someone able to help them think about their experience, however difficult, and to do it in a way which they can accept and believe in.

The attribution of form and meaning to experience by talking about it in a manner which feels sympathetic and true is what then makes it possible to think about experience in order to take it back in again – but as experience which has been thought about, rather than experience which needs to be reacted to or evacuated. We are indebted to the psychoanalyst and writer Wilfred Bion for the idea that learning from experience is dependent upon being able to take it in or absorb it in this way.[3]

This, to my mind, is what getting unstuck is about. Being stuck is usually about having had an experience (or lots of experiences) and finding oneself unable to really think about what has happened; a state of mind which, paradoxically, is often characterised by intense preoccupation or 'over-thinking', but of a claustrophobic kind. There is thinking, but no thinking through.

SIX

Stories we tell ourselves about ourselves, and their truth status. Postmodern 'as if' notions of the truth. What 'as if' therapeutic solutions might look like. Treating reality, in literature, as simply one fiction among many. Delusions and the truth status of delusions: the case of Don Quixote. Quixote's challenge: Is an invented ideal truth sometimes not better than the real truth? The truth status of memories. Historians and how they deal with past (remembered) events. Settler societies and unsettling memories of an often genocidal past.

The patient's story as a subjective truth. Enacting that truth in the consulting room: a case history. Incomplete truths, and the therapist's role in filling out the missing parts. Progression from subjective truth to fuller subjective truth. 'Authenticity' as an alternative term to subjective truth. The importance of holding on to the notion of truth. Truth as process in psychoanalysis (Hanna Segal). The moment of recognition (recognising the truth) in therapy.

❖

JMC – 'The stories we tell about ourselves may not be true, but they are all we have.'

I am interested in our relations with these stories we tell about ourselves, stories that may or may not be true. Let me select three cases.

(a) I have a story about myself which I sincerely believe to be true, in fact which I believe to be the story of me, but which some ideal, omniscient, godlike observer who is entirely independent of me and to whose mind I have no access knows not to be true, or at least not to be the whole truth.

(b) I have a story I tell about myself, one in which I wholeheartedly believe but which certain well-placed observers (my parents, my spouse, my children) know to be flawed, probably self-serving, perhaps even to a degree delusional. (This is a not uncommon state of affairs.)

(c) I have a story about myself in the way that we all have stories about ourselves: I concede that it may not be true by the standards of (a) or even (b); nevertheless, it is 'mine', it is all I have, and therefore I give it my allegiance. 'It's all I have, it's the best I can do.'

I take (c) to describe a common postmodern situation: there is no type (a) ideal observer who holds in their mind the true story of me, therefore let me negotiate some kind of life-narration for myself, one that is prudently enough worked out to take type (b) observers into account, yet that feels honest and sincere, even though I know at the back of my mind that there are interests at work – interests to which I am blind – which have almost certainly dictated that certain parts of 'the' story – the full story, the type (a) story – should be occluded. I will not be able to put my finger on these occluded parts because 'I' am engaged in hiding them from 'myself'.

From my limited acquaintance with the consulting room, I get the feeling that as a discipline psychoanalysis does not take the distinctive features of (c) very seriously. The hyperconscious aspect of (c) is more or less brushed aside as secondary elaboration. Yet my sense is that the type (c) sensibility is more and more common today. It is an expression of the age we live in, and we ought to be cautious about downplaying it.

I may at this point seem to be about to make a plea for a new variety of analysis adjusted to a new personality type, but this is not in fact the direction I want to take. What I wish to focus on is the longing or nostalgia for the one and only truth, a longing that I myself happen to feel strongly, but that I don't see in the kind of contract between therapist and patient which takes it as a premise that all transactions will be on an as-if basis: 'I will tell my story as if it were true, and you will deal with me as if I were not just making it up, and we will see where we can go from there.' (This is a crude version of the contract described in your last communication.)

My first question would be: Starting as if from the truth, where can one expect to arrive, through therapy, save at an as-if destination? My second question would be: Are we truly so changed (so advanced) that we can be satisfied not only by as-if stories but by as-if destinations, by as-if solutions to as-if human plights?

Do therapist and patient nowadays agree to trade only in fictions, fictions that both of them know — with a tacitly suspended knowledge — to be fictions; and is that enough to satisfy them? Or am I in error when I postulate a *them* who are not complexes of fictions but are 'real' human beings whose hunger cannot be satisfied by such ghostly fare?

As you can see, I am as divided, undecided and confused as can be. By profession I have been a trader in fictions. From what I write it must be evident to you that I don't have much respect for reality. I think of myself as using rather than reflecting reality in my fiction. If the world of my fictions is a recognisable world, that is because (I say to myself) it is easier to use the world at hand than to make up a new one. In a letter to Louise Colet, Gustave Flaubert spoke of aspiring to write a book about nothing, a book that would be held together by the mutual tensions of its component parts rather than by its correspondence to any real world. He never wrote such a book: it was much too hard, and anyhow no one would have read it. But it is telling that a writer who is thought of as an arch-realist should have had such a low opinion of reality.

What ties one to the real world is, finally, death. One can make up stories about oneself to one's heart's content, but one is not free to make up the ending. The ending has to be death: it is the only ending one can seriously believe in. What an irony then that to anchor oneself in a sea of fictions one should have to rely on death!

∞

AK – It seems to me that we are talking about two very different kinds of truth. You write about an objective or a transcendent truth, a truth outside or above the realm of human understanding. I am working on the basis of a subjective and an intersubjective truth, a truth to experience, which is what I believe to be at issue when one is trying to help a patient who is suffering. People come for psychotherapy because they feel dreadful and are in subjective distress, not because they do not know if God exists or how to read the weather.

This is not to say that reality – whatever we mean by reality – goes out the window. But in psychotherapy one is not trying to establish objective truth. Instead it is the way the patient represents reality, the way in which the external world exists in the mind of the patient, with its distortions, its inconsistencies, its lapses, which one explores in order to understand the way their mind works and to help deepen their sense of subjective truth.

I would like to present a brief clinical vignette in order to think through this issue in the context of the therapeutic work I am engaged in with patients at the moment.

A male patient started psychoanalytic psychotherapy with me a year and a half ago. He comes three times weekly. This material is drawn from the first session after a long holiday break.

The patient talked about collapsing in the last few

days of the break. He also spoke of missing his sessions very much, particularly at a time when he was fighting with his partner. This patient has always found weekends and holiday breaks difficult. Early on in the therapy he dealt with this by forgetting about what happened in sessions and not thinking about me or the therapy when he was not in the consulting room. I understood this as a defensive manoeuvre, whereby he would do to me what he felt I was doing to him – that is, dropping him from my mind. This made sense to the patient and he called his strategy 'turning the tables'.

At the present point in therapy, things have changed. The patient is more accepting of anxiety he feels about being dependent, which has had a positive impact on relationships in his life, most particularly with his son.

Today he complains bitterly to me about his partner. He has been horrible to her, he says. He does not know why he gets overcome by such rage towards her. The problem on the face of it is a strange one because his partner seems to be very concerned to do all she can to help him, but this only seems to enrage him. At one point he says to me: 'Her love and concern are the problem.'

After a while I talk with him about how he feels vulnerable and needs my help, he needs the help of both his partner and me, but he hates feeling this way.

It makes him feel small. He feels this particularly when he can't come to see me in the break, and therefore feels shut out and rejected. I think when he is horrible to his partner he is getting rid of the feelings of being small and shut out by making his partner feel that way – he is making her feel how he feels. This makes sense to the patient. It draws on many conversations we have had in recent weeks, and has the effect of calming him.

Here I am trying to help the patient develop his tolerance of particular feelings – of needing help and being vulnerable, of feeling anxious about being hurt and rejected – so he does not have to get rid of them by making someone close to him feel them on his behalf.

The vignette describes a fairly standard piece of psychoanalytic work, one in which there is an exploration of feelings that a patient is struggling with inside of himself and the defensive ways he has developed of dealing with them. I hope it also shows the emotional nature of the therapeutic relationship, its significance for the patient, and the way in which one learns about the patient's mind through the direct, lived experience of a relationship with them. It is difficult to get this across when one talks in abstract terms about the **transference**. The patient's story is not some-thing that takes place outside the consulting room and is reported back; it is enacted in a very real way in the relationship with the therapist. The therapist comes to adopt the curious position of being both inside the patient's story and commenting upon it as it unfolds.

In narrative terms we could say that the story changes in the course of the session from something like – 'I feel rage towards my partner who patronises me' – to something like – 'I hate feeling reliant on my partner and my therapist, it makes me feel small and wretched, and when it gets too much I can end up dealing with it by taking it out on them.'

One could characterise what is going on as a swap of one fiction (the patient's) for another (the patient's and mine). But this does not ring true for me. I believe that, like most patients, this one brought his lived experience to me in good faith. It did not have an 'as if' quality about it. It was the truth as he experienced it, although he had enough insight to know that there were aspects to what was going on in his life which he did not understand and which made him and those around him suffer. For my part, I believed in my experience of the relationship with the patient and in what I said to him regarding my understanding of what was going on in his mind.

The aim in psychotherapy is to help the patient fill in parts of a puzzle, which is their puzzle – the puzzle that is their mind. As the situation is considered more fully and one develops, through a shared, lived experience with the patient, an understanding of the impact of the patient's unconscious mind on their conscious experience, one's view of the situation changes – as inevitably as one's view of a small part of a scene alters, sometimes dramatically, when a larger vista is revealed.

I would like to think that, on a good day, the trajectory of a therapeutic session is from a partial subjective truth to a greater subjective truth. I do not think the complete truth can ever be reached.

∞

JMC – Although, like most well brought up people nowadays, I am careful to avoid the impolite locution 'transcendent truth', I confess that privately I continue to distinguish between things that really happened in the past and things that did not really happen. Don Quixote did not couch his lance and charge a giant: he charged a windmill, and if he says he charged a giant then he is lying, or, to put it more usefully, is delusional – is making up a fiction without being aware it is a fiction. The fiction he makes up may be more interesting than the reality, and (as you say) we may be better able to help people like Quixote back to sanity by going along with their stories for a while, pretending to believe they are true, which is what Sancho (who is fond of Quixote) does. Nevertheless, I would resist classing Quixote's story of the giant as truth of any variety, for example, poetic truth or higher truth or transcendent truth or subjective truth. I would prefer to find some other term, one that doesn't lead us into confusion.

Of course patients, when they talk about their past, talk about events only a small part of the time. Mostly they talk about how they thought or felt in the past, how they think or feel in the present about how they thought or felt in the past, how they thought other people were thinking or feeling about them, how they now feel or think about how they thought other people were thinking or feeling about them, and so forth.

Thoughts and memories and feelings are more difficult to conceive as events than is charging a windmill. Is there any hope of recovering what the patient's mother actually said the day she lost her temper with him, when he was six, for putting the cat in the tumble dryer, as distinct from what the patient heard her (when he was six) to be saying and remembers her today as saying, namely, 'You are a cruel and cold-hearted child who is going to grow up to be a cruel and cold-hearted man'? Her utterance was certainly an event, but in practice it is impossible to disentangle it from the interpretation the patient has put upon it many years later. So, I concede, much of the time it would be futile for the therapist to try to distinguish between what actually happened and what the patient thinks happened, and therefore to distinguish between events on the one hand and interpretations of events on the other. In therapy, as you say, the real event, the event that counts, is the event that occurs in the consulting room between the patient and the therapist.

Yet I continue to feel that one takes a step too far if one says to a patient, in effect: 'You have constructed a version of the past which is making you miserable (dysfunctional), so let us work together to construct an alternative version of the past with which you will be happier and which will help you get on with your life.'

The past, individual or collective, is always messier and more complicated than any account we can give of it. We make up an account of the past so that we can pack the past away and not be bothered by its messiness any more. Yet it seems to me a source of hope that historians take it as their calling to, every so many years, lift the accepted account off the shelf and scrutinise it again, checking it against the facts to see whether it still reads like a true account.

Historians are not simple-minded people. Many of them are able to hold two conflicting beliefs in balance: that every account we produce of the past will eventually be revealed to be a story, the kind of story that a man or woman of our times could, in retrospect, have been expected to produce; but that, despite the above, we nevertheless do not have a free hand to make up the past as we wish (or as our times wish us to wish).

It seems to me that the same sort of double awareness ought to colour therapeutic practice.

What is it that holds the historian – or the therapist – to their task? I suppose it is sincere belief in the value of what one is doing. One can't devote oneself heart and soul to a task if one doesn't believe in its value. That is why I would call the double awareness I tried to describe tragic: one believes sincerely in the truth of what one is writing at the same time that one knows it is not the truth.

There is a moment in the second part of *Don Quixote* when Quixote issues a challenge to us. He seems to step outside the reigning delusion that he is a real knight errant and says, in effect: I believe (believe sincerely) in the code of knight-errantry, I act in accord with my beliefs, and I become a better person by so doing. Would you prefer me as I was before – an impoverished member of the Spanish gentry, scraping a living on my run-down estate, waiting for death to come – or as I am now (as I seem to be now) – a protector of the poor and downtrodden, a rescuer of maidens in distress? If you concede that my beliefs transform me for the better, why are you trying to destroy my beliefs?

By the end of the book many of the people around Quixote, particularly Sancho, have given their response to his question: We do indeed prefer the ideal, transformed, better version of you; it may be self-constructed, it may not be 'real', but we are prepared to ignore that detail.

Of course Quixote's companions are not themselves converts to Quixotic idealism, or at least not sincere converts. They are not saying: We vow, all of us, to live out our ideals as you do. Rather, they are saying: The world turns out to be a more lively, more entertaining place when at least some of us live out our ideals (while the rest of us are content to watch).

I am sure that my dogged concentration, here and in earlier exchanges between us, on the ethical dimension of truth versus fiction comes out of my experience of being a white South African who late in life became a white Australian and, in between, lived for years as a white in the United States, where whiteness as a social reality is more masked than in South Africa or Australia but is still there. That is to say, I have lived as a member of a conquering group which for a long while thought of itself in explicitly racial terms and believed that what it was achieving in settling ('civilising') a foreign land was something to be proud of, but which then, during my lifetime, for reasons of a world-historical nature, had to sharply revise its way of thinking about itself and its achievements, and therefore to revise the story it told itself about itself, that is, its history.

Australia is particularly interesting in this regard. Crudely summarised, the story reigning in Australia today is that previous generations of white settlers acted under the sway of the pernicious illusion that because their ancestry was European they were better than indigenous Australians and were therefore justified in subjugating them and taking over their land. However (the story continues) the generations of white Australians who came to maturity after the Second World War underwent some kind of evolution of consciousness as a result of which they have a better and truer understanding of what has really happened in Australia since 1788, that is, have developed a better and truer history of themselves.

In this better and truer history, white Australians today remain the heirs and beneficiaries of a great crime committed by their forebears, the sort of crime which enlightened people like themselves would never themselves commit but which their forebears, slaves to a false conception of themselves and their role in world history, could commit without crippling moral qualms.

If you tell the story of late twentieth-century historical revisionism in these terms, an ambivalence becomes visible which at the level of the individual psyche ought to split people apart and make any kind of easy, happy life impossible. My great-grandparents were criminals (the revised story goes), complicit in an evil project whose fruits I am at present enjoying. Yet at the same time my great-grandparents were courageous, upstanding people who suffered hardship so that their descendants could have a good life.

The story of historical revisionism in Australia is different in scale but not in kind from the story of post-1945 historical revisionism in Germany. Our not so remote ancestors were fine people – so the story goes – but were slaves to an illusion. We ourselves have seen through that illusion. Thus we can see our ancestors as they really were, and our past as it really was. In that very specific sense we are better people than they, or at least freer people, and can set ourselves apart from them.

I am speaking at a level of generality which makes for the crudest of arguments. Nevertheless, let me state my crude point: that the settler societies in question, the settler societies of today, ought to be riven with self-doubt but are not. They – or their more articulate members – say the following: (a) Our forebears did bad things but they are not to be blamed because they were in the grip of false beliefs and a false understanding of their role in history; (b) we have more enlightened beliefs and a more enlightened understanding of our historical role; and (c) if, as history unfolds, we ourselves are revealed to have mistaken ourselves as deeply as our ancestors mistook themselves, there is nothing we can do about that, that is the nature of history, which is just one story overtaking and supplanting another; therefore the best we can do is to get on with our lives without more fretting.

I don't want to push the therapeutic analogy recklessly, so let me simply ask the question: When a society (but for a few dissident members) decides that it does not feel troubled, how can healing even begin?

⌘

AK – I agree, it is hard to imagine healing occurring at a social or an individual level when the prevailing discourse is one that cannot admit to disturbance. I would also suggest that the more determinedly a society feels the need to look upon itself as having risen above the past and as being free and distinct from it, the more likely it is that it will be in history's unconscious sway.

The split awareness you describe in Australia, in which two largely unintegrated pictures of the early settlers coexist, sounds to me like a recipe for collective insecurity. (We have something similar in England, of course, in attitudes towards our colonial past.) In your account Australia's idea of itself as a civilised society seems to rest upon an idealised version of its past, a version in which cruelty and conflict are edited out. This does not sound like the basis for a happy, secure collective life, but an anxious one, in which any experience of well-being is fragile and can easily flip into a more troubled state when it comes up against memories and stories which do not fit with the idealised picture.

Perhaps you are right to say that use of the word truth is confusing in the context of our discussion about psychotherapy because of the implication that truth is a thing that exists out there, like a fact, something which can be possessed or fully understood at any one point in time. I have wondered whether it might be more helpful to invoke the notion of authenticity and of the aspiration to the authentic life, terms from existentialist philosophy which describe the ideal of a life lived through an open response to the experience of being-an-individual-in-the-world. And yet I am reluctant to give up on the idea of subjective or psychic truth. Firstly, I do think people understand what it means: the common instruction 'be true to yourself' gets the message across nicely. But secondly, if it does confuse, I think there may be meaning in the confusion.

To my mind there is something strange and startling about Truth, which exactly captures my experience of discovery in psychoanalysis. Subjective truth in psychoanalysis is not the same as external truth at all, and yet it is something one bumps up against, sometimes quite violently and sometimes more gradually, almost in the manner of an external object or fact. By comparison, authenticity sounds like something you can buy or choose for yourself. It sounds like a lifestyle choice, a serious and not a trivial lifestyle choice, but a choice, something self-willed, nevertheless.

The psychoanalyst Hanna Segal wrote that psychoanalytic truth is a process and not a fact.[4] She was describing the nature of the psychoanalytic endeavour, which is to help the patient understand themselves better by becoming more open to experience, and particularly to unconscious experience, however difficult or painful; and this in the knowledge that complete openness can never be achieved, because psychic life is in its essence dynamic and changing, and defensive processes will always be in operation to a greater or lesser extent. Along with this goes a commitment to a certain way of thinking and being rather than a particular predefined endpoint, although of course the strong hope and expectation is that the process will produce general benefits for the patient as well as a reduction in symptoms. A paradox lies in the fact that while the patient maintains too much of a focus on an endpoint, on, for example, getting rid of a particular symptom, it is much more difficult for them to give themselves to the task of exploring their own mind in a free and open way, and thereby to get to the point where the symptom can be given up.

But I think it is very difficult to properly describe any sort of real encounter with unconscious experience, of the type which occurs at significant moments in psychotherapy, without using the metaphor of an encounter with an aspect of external truth, an object or fact, a Thing. When a patient reaches the point of recognition of something meaningful which was previously not known or known about, it is as if they are saying to themselves: 'Ah now I see, this aspect of things was always there, I can see it now where I couldn't before. I have lived with it for so long but I have found ways of getting round it, or of simply not seeing it, or of pretending it was something else. But now I do see it, as clearly as that chair or table.' It is as if there is some aspect of the internal situation, of which the conscious self was not previously aware, that the psychotherapeutic process brings the patient against, and is then present within the mind where before it was not.

An encounter with something that has previously been unconscious is very like coming up against something outside of oneself, even though it is something that happens inside one's own mind, because this thing or aspect of experience has not been a part of the self before. The situation will not of course remain that way; the find does not have the status of a fact or an object, and will be subject to reshaping and reinterpreting as life continues. But the metaphor still serves to convey the manner in which something important is discovered, uncovered or recovered within the mind.

Does this clarify something of the matter or just add to the confusion?

SEVEN

Authenticity versus sincerity. Settler societies and their racist and/or genocidal past (continued). Mental strategies for denying blame. Present-day Australia and its treatment of asylum seekers. The psychology of doublethink. D. H. Lawrence on genocide, guilt, and the return of the repressed. Repression at the level of the social psyche: instances from Australia. Isabel Menzies Lyth on the development of a social defence system. Coping with conflicting historical accounts: integration or splitting?

Split awareness in the individual and in the social body. Practice example: the forensic nurse who finds it difficult to integrate repulsion at the patient-offender's past actions with developing human sympathies. Ways in which the set-up of the health system can compound the therapist's difficulties. Instance: a health-care system whose defences may be dysfunctional in their logic. Group psychology: theoretical and practical problems. Wilfred Bion on the life of the group.

Obstacles to thinking as a group, to self-reflection within the group.

❖

JMC – I am not sure I would want to do away with the word *authentic* entirely, at least in its negative form. To call an action inauthentic, meaning that it is at odds with the deeper reality of the actor, seems to me to capture a feature of mental life distinct from sincerity: one can sincerely believe in what one is doing even as a keen-eyed outsider can see that at some level one is playing a role, that one is not authentically committed to one's action.

I suspect that the word *authentic* came into wider usage precisely to capture what the word *sincere* fails to – at least in English (in French the word encompasses more than in English). If so, this in turn suggests that the phenomenon of the person who holds a belief in all sincerity yet is not committed heart and soul to that belief is of quite recent birth.

But yes, I agree, practising authenticity, adhering to an ethic of authenticity, does have the ring of a lifestyle choice. Being authentic includes being able to lie and steal and cheat as long as you don't pretend to yourself that you are not a liar and a thief and a cheat. As a society we cut a great deal of slack for 'authentic' characters of this kind. I have never seen why. The classic English novelists (Fielding, Dickens, for example) are often prepared to forgive immorality yet are dead set against hypocrisy, the pretence to virtue.

You suggest that the more a society believes it has cut its ties with the past, the more likely it will at an unconscious level be under the sway of the past. I couldn't agree more. Books could be written on the subject. But cutting ties with the past doesn't quite capture what I was trying to say about South Africa and Australia. To *really* cut your ties with the past is a logical impossibility, since it would mean denying your ancestry and your ancestors, the purest representatives of the past, and in effect claiming to be born anew, out of nothing.

What one actually encounters, in Australia at least, is more interesting. Australians – both those descended from earlier settlers (among whom I include involuntary settlers, i.e. convicts) and those immigrants who, as an act of national affirmation, have accepted a kind of spiritual or adoptive settler descent – do not deny their historical forebears. On the contrary, they are proud of them. Yet at the same time they attribute to these same forebears a viciousness and cruelty toward the aboriginal dwellers on the land of which they themselves would never be guilty.

The forebears I refer to are not at all remote in time: an Australian of middle age is likely to have had grandparents whose attitudes toward, and beliefs about, people of colour would be found to be, in the reigning euphemism, inappropriate, that is to say, unacceptable or even repellent.

How then do ordinary Australians square pride in their ancestry with rejection of what those ancestors sincerely believed in? Part of the answer is that they achieve it by invoking the notion of the Zeitgeist. In the old times, the time of the ancestors – so goes the Zeitgeist story – racism was in the air as a sort of miasma that invaded everyone's lungs. Inhaling it involuntarily, our ancestors became, willy-nilly, racists; but not racists in a real sense, as Hitler (say) was a racist. Their racism was not an active, conscious racism. They caught it in much the same way that one catches flu; it was no more part of their being than flu would be. By the standards of today – of today's Zeitgeist – our ancestors may seem morally defective. But moral standards change and evolve with time – there is nothing we can do about that (the story continues). As our moral standards today seem good to us, so no doubt their moral standards seemed good to them. Therefore while from our vantage point, within our Zeitgeist, we rightly reject their standards, it would be unfair (unjust) to reject our ancestors themselves, caught as they were in their own Zeitgeist, for being exponents of those standards.

I recently watched an adaptation for television of one of the stories that make up my book *Elizabeth Costello*. Gazing around a gathering, Elizabeth asks herself how it can possibly be true that her fellow citizens are participants in a shadowy compact (shadowy in the sense that its operations are shielded from public view) to slaughter living beings and devour their flesh. May the truth not rather be that there is something wrong with her, that she has somehow become possessed by a perverse will to see evil where there is none?

Elizabeth's frame of mind is all too familiar to me. How can

my good, kindly neighbours be descended from people who justified the slaughter of other living beings on the grounds that they
were not fully human? More to the point, how can I myself be
descended from such people? Is the truth not more likely to be
that there is something wrong with me and my thinking, that in
an overdelicate way I am refusing to accept that notions of good
and bad change with time, that morality is what the etymology
of the word hints that it is: simply a set of mores, of folk-ways?
Am I not merely being morbid?

I write not in a cool, scientific spirit but under the sway of feeling.
Specifically I write in the aftermath of a decision by the Australian
parliament to revise its legislation on asylum seekers. The new
legislation threatens the draconian penalty of indefinite detention on
some hellhole of an island for people who fail to follow the prescribed
procedure for claiming asylum – namely, filling in a form at a refugee
centre somewhere abroad and taking their place in a long queue –
and instead choose to pay a shady smuggler a hefty fee to transport
them as near as he can get to the Australian mainland.

The penalty is purposely and explicitly out of all proportion
to the offence because it is meant to deter the practice of seeking
asylum by 'illegal' (more accurately, extra-procedural) means.
News of the new, callous approach is intended to be relayed to
Afghanistan and Sri Lanka and other countries from which people
are fleeing that trying the 'illegal' route is not worth the candle,
that they are better off staying at home.

One can with the utmost confidence say that in a generation or two Australian schoolchildren will be reading in their history books that in the early twenty-first century their ancestors tried all means, fair and foul, to block the tide of Asian immigration to Australia, and generally behaved in an inappropriate (i.e. inhuman) fashion. Fortunately, their history books will continue, the Zeitgeist changed and a more enlightened outlook came to prevail. Thus we should not be overhasty, the lesson will conclude, to condemn our ancestors: they were simply children of their times.

The rhetorical strategy of this imaginary history book is the same strategy we use today: we set limits to the moral capacities of the ancestors, making them, in effect, the unevolved, unenlightened ones, the children, while we become the adults.

As a moral critique of a strategy of doublethink, what I am saying is more or less clear. What I am still struggling to do is to place the strategy in a psychological framework. The strategy must have a psychological dimension, since as a piece of self-deception it works: it enables us to retain our good opinion of ourselves yet not to unmoor ourselves entirely from the past. To some extent it follows the outline of the family romance: these unacceptable people are not my parents, my true parents are much nicer (more presentable). But further than that I haven't been able to go. Perhaps it is always a mistake to try to transfer features of individual psychology to the psychology of the collective.

Can you help?

∞

AK – It may be a logical impossibility to imagine being born out of nothing, being without origins or history, but it is not a psychic impossibility.

What you describe in Australian society is a split view of the way the settler-forebears behaved towards the Aboriginal people. This is one in which a benign, idealised picture of the settlers predominates, presenting them as noble pioneers who only behaved as they did (if one goes along with this version one finds oneself speaking euphemistically) because this was how people did things in those days; because, in other words, they were products of their time. Awareness of another version, one in which the white settlers dealt out immense and shocking cruelty and suffering to the Aboriginal people, is split off and remains relatively inaccessible to public consciousness. The truth, as I see it, does not reside in one version or another, but in some sort of integration of the two.

It is usual with such a split for most members to hold the predominant, benign view of their forebears most of the time, but for a minority of members to be left to hold a morbid preoccupation with another, more disturbing version. A split in understanding something of real importance to a social body is, I think, what produces subversion or an underground movement.

The purpose of the split is, as you say, to preserve a link with the past; but a link of a certain, rather unhelpful type. This idealised link, which is of course based on an identification with the more positive aspects of one's ancestry, obviates the need for those in the present to engage in a fuller and closer way with the more threatening and negative aspects of their history. It is no surprise you have to remind me how recently these events took place because it is as if they have been consigned to the pages of a dusty history book, distanced by history from the present.

The problem is set out in your account of recent developments in immigration law in Australia. If one's knowledge of history as a social body hinges upon airbrushing out those aspects which are unpalatable, which involve in this case a widespread, cruel and inhuman disregard for another people with whom one is attempting to share territory, then one will not be addressing a key problem in the present. This is a problem which is not consigned to history but is continually faced by our species, and centres on the question of how we share the resources of our planet in the context of a rapidly rising world population, human conflict and natural disaster. In fact one could be said to be working hard not to address it, and as a consequence the chances of repetition, of renewed cruelty and inhumanity, will be high.

Let me turn to a much smaller-scale example from my work to try to explore the matter further. Ten years ago I carried out a series of exploratory research interviews with staff working in forensic mental health services to better understand the impact of work in a challenging and complex environment. These staff were working closely with male offenders with a diagnosis of personality disorder: men who had long-term and pervasive psychological difficulties and who had committed pretty terrible crimes, usually of a sexual or violent nature.

The interviews showed clearly how split staff's views of patient-offenders were, how difficult staff found it to bring together in their minds the patient with the offender: the vulnerable man who inspired sympathy, concern and often affection, with the man who had done terrible things to vulnerable people. They described with anguish how hard it was to reconcile this split and how it felt to live with this double awareness. Here is a nurse trying to put this into words:

> Sometimes I think I should be less assertive with him because you know he comes across as somebody who's very vulnerable and very weak . . . and all the time you think 'Well you're telling me you're not an angry person, you're passively sitting here, yet you've killed someone really extremely violently', and you know everything contradicts in your mind: the behaviours you see . . . knowing what they've actually done, how violent their offending can be and how they're actually presenting to you . . . it was almost like playing games, nothing seems real on the ward.

The rehabilitative task, of course, is to weigh things up: to help forensic patients get a grip on how their deep-seated problems in relationships, their ways of dealing with their own traumas and vulnerabilities, led them to victimise other people. To help patients do this, staff have to be able to do it too: they have to be able to make real sense of the fuller picture, of the relationship between the victim and the victimiser in the person they see in front of them.

From my research I became convinced that the way in which services for this particular patient group are set up in the UK, the isolation of such services, as well as the way in which they are configured internally, left ground-level staff in an invidious position. Staff's difficulty in integrating their view of patients was best understood, not as a problem originating in the patient, or as a problem originating in staff, but as a product of an interaction between a difficult human task and an unsupportive and uncomprehending environment. As an example of this, staff spoke about how isolated they were, both within society (a prevailing attitude of hostility was felt towards patients and staff) and the wider hospital environment, and in consequence how heavy was their reliance on their own small, tightly knit team. This meant they were highly reluctant to point out to colleagues when a relationship with a patient was becoming too close or too negative in some way, even though they knew full well how important it could be to do so.

These staff felt cut off in mental and physical terms from society, thrown together behind locked doors with a small group of colleagues and patients. No wonder that relationships could become intense and claustrophobic, no wonder that it was so hard for these staff to find perspective on their situation in either therapeutic or human terms.

This type of social situation, in which things are organised in a protective fashion at one point in time (protecting the public, in this case, from people who frighten them) but end up obstructing an important task (reducing the risk of these people reoffending), is symptomatic of what Isabel Menzies Lyth called a **social defence system**.[5] The system develops a life of its own, one in the face of which individuals eventually feel quite powerless. They can long to reach a fuller, more integrated understanding, to make their society better and more inclusive, but the way things are set up, the rules, the procedures, the types of relationships that are possible, militate strongly against this.

Do these ideas have any relevance to the situation you describe in Australia?

∽

JMC – Let me hasten to say that I would not want to confine my remarks on colonial genocides to Australia – far from it.

Your comments on split responses – acknowledging and denying at the same time – lead me to think of what D. H. Lawrence had to say about colonisation and its psychic aftermath.[6] In a 1923 essay on the novelist James Fenimore Cooper, Lawrence writes to the following effect: The Aztecs and Incas have been annihilated, the Eskimos and Patagonians and 'Red Indians' have been reduced to manageable numbers and will never recover the lands that were once theirs. As long as the Indians were a credible foe, the settlers were immune from 'the daimon, or demon, of America'. But now that the last nuclei of Indian life have broken up, the descendants of the colonial conquerors will have to reckon with that demon and the full force of its psychic onslaught.

As a prophet Lawrence (here) doesn't convince me: the United States may be haunted by its slaveholding past, but I see little sign among Americans of a guilty awareness that the land they tread on is stolen. What interests me in Lawrence's comments is their diagnostic aspect: that once the aboriginal owners of the land have been exterminated or rendered null, they (so to speak) invade and take possession of the psyche of the conqueror as a malign inner force, in a literal return of the repressed. Thus, as Lawrence sees it, there are two phases to colonial conquest. In the first phase, the aboriginal is treated in an unambivalent way as the enemy, to be hunted and killed. In the second (and presumably guilt-haunted) phase, the ghost-demon of the annihilated aboriginal enters the colonial psyche, which then splits and wars upon itself.

Methodologically, there seems to me a huge gap to bridge between processes of repression and splitting in the individual psyche and similar processes in the collective (I hesitate to write 'collective mind' or 'collective psyche', such concepts having been severely questioned). But I think that if one uses the psychoanalytic insight as nothing more than a metaphor, without pretending to be doing actual psychoanalysis, there is much to be gained by thinking about a society that, at least in its public discourse, does its best to avoid topics it finds uncomfortable, and does its best to sanction and silence people who dredge them up from the past.

So, to give a highly simplified example, it has become difficult in our day, in a country like Australia, to ask the simple question of whether people – namely our ancestors – who did bad things were themselves bad people. The response from the public, or from the spokespersons of the public, tends to be a lengthy one: (a) It is important to acknowledge the mistakes of the past and even (b) to apologise for them; however, at the same time (c) we should not dwell on the past, but (d) move on. A more sophisticated version of the same response might even refer us to Freud on mourning and melancholia: it is right and good to mourn the tragic events of our history, but sorrow and regret and feelings of guilt, which are normal human responses to such events, must nevertheless be worked through, otherwise we become stuck in an unprofitable melancholia.

In the Australian response there may even be an added tinge of impatience and irritation: Why do these people (i.e. Aboriginal people) go on and on about the past and about the wrongs done to them? The past is past, there is nothing we can do to change it, so why don't they buckle down and get on with their lives?

On your advice, I had a look at the essay by Isabel Menzies Lyth on hospital nurses, and found it fascinating. Though I have never worked in a hospital, I have worked in organisations (offices, teaching departments, even briefly a high school) where I was struck by how **regressive** the culture of the collective, and how primitive the passions in play at the communal level, can be – in contrast to the maturity and sophistication of individual members. ('Culture' is not a term you or Menzies Lyth use, but it seems to have taken over the field by now.)

I can well understand how the objective activity of working with offenders – as you have done in forensic hospitals – or of taking care of patients in regular hospitals can give rise to high levels of unconscious anxiety and provoke the erection of defence mechanisms of the kind that you and Menzies Lyth describe. The point I would want to focus on, however, is the collusion that allows the defences of individuals to be incorporated into a group defence system, which will then evolve its own apparatus of sanctions to deal with newcomers who don't join up – who don't, to use Menzies Lyth's term, **introject** the defence system.

Menzies Lyth writes of the 'collusive interaction between individuals to project and reify relevant elements of the psychic defence system'. I try to imagine how this collusion might take place. Might some leader emerge, for example, who sets a precedent and exerts pressure on the others to follow the precedent; or might the process be more intuitive, more like what we might tentatively call the operation of a collective psyche?

However these collusive interactions take place, I think it is important to chart their evolution and their workings. I don't know whether, when good news is spread, it is spread by what amounts to collusive interaction; but when malign rumours are spread, my intuition is that collusive interaction is often the mechanism used. One has only to think of the schoolyard, and of how it mysteriously comes about that a particular child comes to be targeted for shunning. My guess is that Menzies Lyth would say that collusive interaction applies only to the spread of the malignant, because the process is essentially regressive (which may be why groups strike one as more primitive than the individuals who make them up).

I would like to see an observational study of group regression: how a defence system within an institution like a hospital or a health service is born and evolves, how its norms are imposed on or absorbed by entrants to the group. There are novelists who describe the workings of gossip very well: how it acts to exclude its victims from society, and how hard it is to go against the tide. Jane Austen is one such novelist, Patrick White another.

The Roman poets saw gossip or public opinion as a supernatural or at least eerie force, under the name *fama*.

To sum up, then: What I would like to know is how, at the theoretical level, one gets from the individual to the group – how one would generalise from the individual psyche to the group psyche. Does it make any sense to speak of a group psyche, or is it better to restrict oneself to speaking about a set of practices followed by the group, sustained by individual psychic processes that somehow act in concert?

In this connection I would want to question your suggestion

that, when one is faced with two conflicting judgments on past events (e.g. that settlement of Australia was a benign process, that settlement of Australia was a cruel business), one should strive for 'some sort of integration of the two'. There is integration and there is integration. If the two accounts really conflict – and, of course, if you have an emotional investment in them – then there can be no overarching account that erases the conflict – no brown, so to speak, that is neither red nor green but results from putting red and green together. Integration must be possible – we would all be half-mad, split creatures if it were not – but how one achieves it and gets to 'the truth' I can't quite see. All that I see at the moment is the infant and the breast. The breast is good, the breast is bad: two conflicting judgments. How can it (it?) be both good and bad at the same time? What is the truth about it? Isn't that where the splitting begins?

∞

AK – You want to know how you get from a psychology of the individual to a psychology of the group. It seems logical to start at the level of the individual and work upwards, but I'm not sure this is the most fruitful approach. Perhaps it's better to work from experiences of group life, from its particular qualities and products – although this is intrinsically extremely difficult to do. The reason, I think, is that one cannot do it satisfactorily as an individual; or at least one has to wrestle with the problem of how an individual mind works at understanding a plurality of minds or a group entity. We are all members of groups, and have experiences of being in groups. But we can by definition only know about them as individuals, as a small part of a whole.

Isabel Menzies Lyth wrote that it takes a group to study a group.[7] I understand this to mean that as individuals we tend to identify quite narrowly with other individuals, and that thinking about the complexity of group life becomes more possible when minds come together to work upon the issue and there are a number of identifications to draw upon.

I would think that one of the reasons the psychology of groups matters to you is because you were brought up in the apartheid era in South Africa and have witnessed first-hand the consequences of wide-scale group regression. I, on the other hand, have grown up in relative peace and stability in Britain. I was not born into one of the more shameful chapters of British history. (Although now, in this savage era of high capitalism, I sometimes think that a silent civil war is taking place, a war in which profit and individual greed are pitted firmly against social and communal values.)

My interest in group life originates from work in forensic hospitals where I repeatedly saw well-meaning and well-trained staff behaving in the most thoughtless and inhuman ways towards patients. The culture in these places was oppressive too; there was a strong atmosphere in one of the hospitals where I worked, and a powerful experience of leaving one's personal, non-work identity at the locked doors of the institution to become one of the group. Staff enjoyed this sense of surrender, of being relieved of selfhood, as well as finding it troubling.

I've developed a group learning task on the training course in clinical psychology where I work to help trainees learn about organisational cultures in public health services in the UK. They carry out detailed hour-long observations in a variety of settings within local NHS services (these are almost always observations of staff and patient groups), bringing observational material to a supervision group for help in making sense of it. They are asked to look afresh at whatever it is they observe, and to be curious about everything going on around them, as well as paying particular attention to their own reactions to the situation and their feelings during the observational hour.

Our supervision groups only meet four times, whereas on psychoanalytic trainings such groups meet for as long as two years. It is still fascinating to see how the clinical psychology trainees use the supervision groups to extend their understanding of what is going on in a particular ward or service, moving from a position of sympathising with one particular subgroup or individual to an engagement with a wider social dynamic. A typical pattern is for the trainees to side with patients against staff, shocked at the failures of care and compassion they witness on understaffed and under-resourced wards. Discussion in the group opens things up: someone starts to think more deeply about what life is like for staff on the ward, or for a particular person who has captured their attention in some way, making links with their own experience of work on a similar ward or unit. Figures who at first appeared two-dimensional begin to acquire a third dimension, and the trainee returns for a second observation with an altered mindset.

My sense is that to begin to understand an aspect of group culture one has to rise above identifications with individuals and to observe what is happening at a group level, finding words for the kind of group one is interested in, its purpose (this is often unclear and masked by a false sense of purpose), and the struggles it faces. Terms need to be found to describe what is observed, and I think we have – certainly in the Anglo-Saxon world – a far less developed language for group experience than for that of the individual.

Wilfred Bion's view was that groups had their own life, their own dynamic, which ought not to be reduced to the terms of an individual psychology. He is very amusing on the subject in the papers collected in his volume *Experiences in Groups*.[8] He writes of the first meeting of a group he has been invited to 'take', the aim of which is to learn about group life. He describes how irrelevant, strange and absurd his comments about how he is being treated as a potential leader of the group come across to the individual members of the group. But he nevertheless powerfully conveys the strong and confused desire for a leader projected onto him by the group before the group has even the first idea of what they are doing and of how they might go about doing it.

One of the reasons why group behaviour can get so out of control, why group dynamics can be so powerful and destructive, is that it is so difficult to think properly as a group. For a group to reflect on itself as a group is a considerable achievement. A group or a society that wants to find a way to consider its manner of functioning, that is curious about itself, has to first find some sort of agreement for doing so amongst its members and to then decide upon and develop structures and procedures to support reflexive activity. What one sees time and time again is groups courageously attempting to do this, but falling prey to a repetition of problematic behaviour. The fiercely hierarchical group has meeting after meeting in which underlings are simply told what to do, the group in which managers and staff do not talk to each other arranges to meet, but separately. In other words, the coordination of the activity of thinking about a group is a task in itself.

An individual has only to consider themselves – and that, of course, can be difficult enough!

EIGHT

Group experiences: music, football, ecstatic religion. Shared 'knowledge' within the group. Theoretical problems about group thought. The individual versus the group: personal experience in South Africa. Nationalism as regressive group experience. Bion on group thinking. Eugène Marais on the collective soul. The experience of being born into a large (extended) family. The nature of group activity, past and present-day. Group labour and alienation. Voluntary versus involuntary group membership. School classes as groups. Regressive behaviour in the classroom. Childhood gangs.

Positive, non-regressive aspects of nationalism. Understanding group mentality. The neonate's experience of the group. The family triad as fundamental group. The National Health Service as collective endeavour. Alienation within the present-day NHS. The family as training ground for success in the group. Oedipal development. The depressive position (Klein) as it impacts on group life. 'Triangular space' (Ronald Britton) and accommodation of the self to the group. Consequences of failure to attain the third position.

❖

JMC — I switched on the radio the other day, and there was someone playing the Goldberg Variations. It was an interesting performance, I thought, a little too romantic for my taste, but thoughtful and engaging. Then I heard a subdued cough, and realised it was a live performance, or at least a recording of a live performance. So, alone at home, I was listening to music in the company, or perhaps just the recorded company, of a group of strangers.

I could not see these fellow listeners, had no idea where they lived, who they were as individuals, but there was something obvious uniting us: we were prepared to drop other business in order to listen to (as it turned out) Angela Hewitt. We were gathered to hear a pianist whom we knew and admired as she exposed herself to the music, and through her we were in turn exposing ourselves to it, letting it take us over. For the duration of the performance we were, so to speak, one soul, united in — I can't find a better word — love. From our communal body — and, bear it in mind, we were not all in the same physical space — there flowed a love directed through the priestly performer, bent over the keyboard, to Johann Sebastian, and beyond him to whoever or whatever directed his hand. And of course through the music we felt some sort of love flowing toward us (otherwise why would we have been there?).

Then the piece ended and there was a long, long silence before anyone dared to clap.

What I have described is a group experience, an experience in which one's ego awareness is suppressed or dwindles away. The world seems all of a sudden uncomplicated. One is *at one* with one's neighbours, in a state of mild ecstasy, outside of one's everyday self.

There is a less high-minded version of group ecstasy to be seen in the football crowd. Some people go to football games less to watch the football than to have the crowd experience – except, of course, that the crowd is constituted, given unity, by the intense focus of its individual members on a single, deeply engaging event, namely the contest on the pitch.

If one is hostile to the phenomenon of the crowd, one speaks of it as a mob, from *mobile vulgus*, the street rabble whose passions are mobile, easily stirred, unpredictable. There is such a thing as crowd or mob psychology, but whether it is useful to speak about that in the same breath as the psychology of the individual is open to question. The fact is, there are people who do not enjoy being alone, feel it as a kind of oppression, feel that they come properly alive when they are with other people, in a group or even a crowd. As a society we elect to punish people by locking them up by themselves, so there must be some sort of social consensus that being alone for long stretches is not pleasant.

You express your own doubts about whether it is possible or

profitable to make the transition from individual psychology to what we are, in a loose way, calling group psychology. I would certainly agree that it is difficult to use the psychology of the individual as a way to understand the 'psychology' of the crowd, just as the psychology of the individual does not help us to understand ecstatic states in general, since ecstatic states are a matter of escaping from or abandoning the self.

But you pose the question in a deeper form: How can we know about groups *as groups*, as opposed to knowing about them as pluralities of individuals? And, invoking Menzies Lyth, you suggest that a group may often arrive at a better understanding of another group than any solitary inquirer can.

If we think about groups at crowd level or even larger, there is indeed a sense in which groups know about other groups, though as intellectuals we have a near-visceral mistrust of such knowledge. I am thinking about the way in which neighbouring nations or tribes with a long history of conflict behind them know about each other. Because they are neighbours they know a great deal of ordinary stuff about each other; but their knowledge or knowingness is more often than not coloured or tainted with a kind of generalising prejudice (the Scots are tight-fisted, the English are treacherous, and so forth) which is not amenable to reason: it is, so to speak, part of the culture and therefore unquestionable.

Our inclination as intellectuals is to deny that this sort of knowledge is proper knowledge. But since it is expressly regarded as knowledge by its holders ('We know the Scots in a way that you don't, we have lived cheek by jowl with them since the beginning of history') we should be wary of discounting it.

A further word of caution. Ecstatic states have been part of religious experience in religions all over the world. There are ecstatic variants of Christianity (too many to name), of Judaism (the Hasidim), of Islam (the Sufis). The 'high' or rational variants of these religions tend to look down on the ecstatic variants as regressive, as a yielding or return to a primitive way of gaining access to the divine. I think we should be wary of importing this 'high' prejudice against the non-rational (the 'irrational') into our reflections on group psychology, of assuming from the beginning that group psychology must be 'primitive' and therefore uncomplicated.

Of course your own interest, professional and personal, is in groups smaller than crowds. You note that groups are often better understood by other groups, such as study groups, than by individual researchers; and you go on to write very interestingly about the psychic dynamics within the research group. You observe that, at least in the Anglo-Saxon tradition, the technical language to describe group phenomena is underdeveloped.

My own sense – for which I can provide no backing whatsoever – is that more communal cultures than our own – for example, traditional African cultures – have a better conceptual apparatus than ours to cover this field, and are better at thinking about group phenomena than we are. Unfortunately, we can't import such a conceptual apparatus without importing the whole culture, the whole *Weltanschauung*, with it.

You suggest that my interest in how groups think may stem from the fact that I grew up in apartheid-era South Africa.

That may indeed be true; but the evolution of my interest does not follow as straight a path as may seem from the outside. The tribe or people into which I was born, the Afrikaners, with which I had an intense tussle, particularly during my childhood, certainly had, at least during the twentieth century – it is less true now – a strong sense of needing to hold together as a group against a hostile world, and a tendency to class people as either with them or against them, with no gradations in between. A more complex relationship with the group, such as the one I had (and have), was ruled out.

Although there was pressure from above, from the more ideological element in the leadership, for organised displays of patriotism or groupthink – for mass rallies or military displays, for instance, such as one associates with Nazi Germany – I never detected much enthusiasm for these among ordinary Afrikaners. One should not forget that Afrikaners had their finest hour during the Anglo-Boer War, when they managed to put together an irregular yet highly effective fighting force characterised far more by individualism than by group discipline: men (I hesitate to call them soldiers) felt it was their right to quit the battle lines, saddle their horses, and ride home to their families for the weekend. As a way of life, militarism invites us to discard the individual faculty of judgment, to submit to overriding group passions. Calvinism, the official religion of the Afrikaner state, was and is a religion of reason, suspicious of irrational forces. That is the main reason why the Calvinist churches in South Africa are steadily bleeding to death, as they lose members to the charismatics.

So my childhood quarrel with Afrikanerdom was not with a system that sought to engulf everyone, including me, in its irrationalism (an example of such a system might be Maoism), but with Afrikaner triumphalism: the values of the Afrikaner petite bourgeoisie, including its virulent prejudices, dominated public discourse, and if you raised the mildest voice of dissent you would be smitten aside.

My own family certainly provided me, struggling as I was like all children to understand my place in the world, with puzzling moral material. I think most immediately of my mother, whose relations with other human beings at a personal level were (I thought) morally admirable but who was nevertheless a supporter, if not of apartheid as a social system, then certainly of the people who ran the country. (My mother was 'not political' in the sense in which most people are 'not political': they identify with leaders rather than policies.) In the case of people like my mother one can certainly speak of regressions, and corresponding returns, that took place as she fluctuated between being her own self and being a white South African.

Thus, to state the thesis baldly that is implicit in what I have been saying: nationalism (tribalism) is a regressive state; and if groups (group thought, group behaviour) are a concern of mine, it is because, over the course of a lifetime, at some cost, I have, reactively, withheld myself from regression to the group.

At some cost because I think regression is a natural part of human life. I would even go so far as to say that periodic regression may be part of the natural psychic economy, part of the way in which we stay healthy (stay 'balanced').

It barely needs to be said that Wilfred Bion was interested in groups because the world around him had between 1914 and 1918 regressed into a group madness whose maddest feature was an appearance of extreme rationality (example: military planning). As you observe, it always has been difficult to think as a group; and it may indeed be necessary, you imply, to elaborate a proper technical language before one can begin to talk about group thinking. In this respect one might start by reflecting on the very notion of thinking. Is it a good idea to use the same word for what individuals do and what the group does? What is it we do when we think we are thinking?

A further footnote on the genesis of my interest in group thought. A generation after Gustave Le Bon (whom Freud read carefully) began to explore crowd psychology, an Afrikaner named Eugène Marais published a book about termite colonies whose thesis is that the colony has a single, collective mind.[9] Marais made it clear that this single mind was not to be understood metaphorically: it was indeed a mind, transcending the sum of the intelligences of the individual termites. Marais, poet, medical doctor and footloose intellectual, also wrote a book about the moment in evolutionary history when the individual conscious-ness separates out from the group.

∞

AK – It sounds almost as if you associate any strong sense of belonging to a group with regression. But of course many of the greatest human achievements are the result of groups working together and developing, as a result of this, a strong sense of a shared identity. The audience at a concert or the crowd at a foot-ball match may be enjoying a relatively uncomplicated group experience, feeling at one with a larger body and taken out of themselves and beyond the bounds of individual selfhood. But the team on the pitch or the musicians in the orchestra will be working hard, and, in contrast with their audience, working up against the limits of selfhood, acting through an understanding of their small part in a complex whole – or at least attempting to do so.

By the same token, I do not think nationalism is a form of regression per se. There is a distinction to be made between a national group that feels a well-deserved sense of pride in its achievements and the sort of nationalist sentiment or jingoism that is motivated by the need to bolster one's own side by putting another side down – often through acts of intimidation and aggression. As you point out, this type of nationalism tends to be accompanied by an extreme intolerance of dissent from within. But real or rightful national pride ought to be the basis for better relations within and between peoples, not worse.

Your comments above have led me to rethink what I wrote about it being useful to consider a group as a group rather than a plurality of individuals. I still think there is some value in this idea from a technical point of view. I have been impressed by the skill with which group and family therapist colleagues have observed and understood what is going on in the consulting room at a group level, rather than getting drawn in by the experience of an individual or a small set of individuals within the group. And I have already mentioned Bion, who wrote about tendencies in the ways the early psychotherapeutic groups he ran after the First World War related to him as a leader, demonstrating the powerful and altogether unfounded expectations the groups had of him: expectations which would not necessarily have been in the mind of any one individual in the group, but were communicated forcefully to him by the way the group behaved as a whole.

However, the conclusion that should *not* be drawn from this type of observation, and most particularly the observation that the attitude of the group is not present in any straightforward way in the minds of individuals within the group, is that the group is one thing and the individuals in the group are another. It is easy to fall into this trap because the two can seem so far apart. In my training role, for example, colleagues and I often share an observation along the following lines: 'That group of students is so difficult, but get them on their own and it is a completely different thing.'

It seems to me that when a group is acting on the basis of contributions which individual members know about, upon which they have real and conscious purchase, there is one situation, akin to a well-functioning democracy in national life, where individual and group life are experienced as firmly connected. But the alternative situation often prevails, in whole or in part, a situation in which a group acts in ways that are almost beyond comprehension to the individuals within it – or to many of them at least. In this case group behaviour could be understood as the outcome of the contributions of all the individuals within the group, however large or small, but many of these individuals are not conscious either of the nature of the contribution they have made or the fact of their having made it. Individual experience and the mentality and behaviour of the group of which the individual is a part can feel very disconnected. This does not mean that they *are* disconnected, but just that we need to work to understand the nature of the relationship between them.

The challenge, the social and the psychological task, to my way of thinking, is for individuals to develop their understanding of their part in the group, their part in the whole, and for the group, large or small, to help them to do this.

I find it helpful to go back to the beginnings of life, to the birth of a baby in a family, to better understand the nature of the task for the individual of establishing a relationship with a group. A baby is born, and what we know is that from the very beginning the infant is utterly dependent on its mother or main carer, and acutely aware of her presence, and also her absence – the whole business of waiting and wanting to be fed or cleaned or held. But recent infant observation research has also highlighted the intense interest shown by infants in the plurality of relationships into which they are born – the voices of parents and siblings in the womb, the tenor and feel of the parental relationship and of mother's other social relationships. What I imagine is that we all begin to form ideas in our mind from very early on about the social group into which we are born, about the nature of the relationships within it, and about our place in relation to it.

Bringing to mind a baby's first experiences of family and social life focuses attention on particular features of the individual's relation to the group, which include the extent to which we depend upon it for life, succour and stimulation, and the fact that it brings us up against the limits of our own significance. We are only one of a number. There are relationships from which we are excluded, and even those we love most turn their attention away from us, and see things differently, sometimes extremely differently, from the way we do. It is all rather disturbing, but crucial I think in order to begin to make some sense of what is going on in groups – or I should say, in individuals in a group situation – at a primitive level.

The smallest group number, as far as I am concerned, is three. This is because for a group to be a group there must be at least one relationship from which any individual is potentially excluded – upon which they might or might not rely, which might or might not offer help and support, but which is, at least potentially, outside their direct experience and control. The familiar saying 'Two is company, three is a crowd' expresses very well, I think, the essential ambivalence we feel towards the group.

⁓

JMC – My first thought, reading what you had to say about being born, was: 'Born into a group? Surely not! Surely a family is not the same kind of thing as a group!'

At the moment of birth one is expelled, protesting all the while, from a sensual paradise into a hostile world where, as it turns out, there will be only a single protective presence, and a not entirely reliable one: the mother. At least so it seems to me; and so it seemed to Freud too, if I am not mistaken.

The idea that the world is fundamentally hostile to the neonate may seem paranoid but it is not entirely fantastic. In the animal world, after all, the helpless newborn are the choice prey of predators.

Thus the act of *being born into* may not be as simple a matter as you say: the group may resist and even be hostile to a new entrant.

My second, more reflective response is the following: Must the field of forces into which the child emerges always be defined by the triangle of mother, father, and babe? While the triangle may seem the right way to talk about firstborn children, or children born into small nuclear families, might it not be odd to apply the triangle to, say, a tenth child born not only to a mother and father but almost as immediately to a milling crowd of brothers and sisters and grandparents and cousins and aunts and uncles – a tenth child whose first intellectual task in the world must be to work out who all these people are, which of them are relevant and which irrelevant to his/her welfare? In other words, to a theorist whose picture of the family is based on what families have been like at most times in history and in most human societies, as opposed to a theorist whose picture of the family is of mother and father plus 2.1 children, the experience of entering (being born into) a family might be much like that of entering a large group of strangers; the most immediate feature of the group (as opposed to the nuclear family) being that you are not the centre of the group's attention, and indeed may have to exert all your tiny powers to be so much as noticed.

Here I am simply going over ground that you have already covered.

You are much less severe on nationalism than I am. I concede, I see little good in it, even when it confines itself to celebrating the achievements of the nation-group. When nations are not defining themselves in terms of a common birth or ancestry (*nation* from *nascor*, to be born), which in practice has meant in terms of race, they define themselves *as against* other nations, that is to say, they base their claim to a common identity on a negative quality (we Icelanders are not Danes, we Pakistanis are not Indians, and so forth). In this respect the negatively defined nation is different from a faith, where group identity rests on shared beliefs and observances, or from a craft guild, where it rests on each member having passed a set of tests.

Whereas my life-experience of nationalism has been mainly unfortunate, yours seems to have been fairly benign. That may be enough to explain our difference in outlook. If you and I were historians, your starting point would be that nationalism can be a force for the good, while mine would be that the rhetoric of nationalism is a disguise for darker drives. From these opposed starting points we could proceed to construct opposed readings of history, different in outlook but perfectly acceptable as contributions to the wider historical debate.

But we are not historians, and both of us, I think, would want to explore our differences more deeply. Thus, for instance, you might object that it is not good enough to proceed from the premise that whenever one joins a group one regresses psychologically, since that premise is unexamined. And anyhow, as you point out, how can the group always be more primitive (and therefore stupider) than the individual when so many of the greatest human achievements have been the handiwork of groups? (I presume you have something like the great cathedrals of Europe at the back of your mind.)

So let me try to set out some initial thoughts on groups – on group membership and group achievements.

(1) Some group projects – transformations of the physical landscape such as the damming of rivers or the terracing of

hillsides – have been heroic achievements that have made life easier for generations afterwards. Particularly in pre-mechanical times, these reworkings of the face of the earth could only be brought about by the joint efforts of huge numbers of people working in a disciplined way according to a single plan. About such hierarchically organised projects I would simply observe that most participants did not volunteer for the job, and that while they got to follow orders they never got to give them.

(2) Computer software systems such as Windows are never the work of a single mind. The writing is conceived from the beginning as a team project and is organised in modular fashion: the projected system is broken down into a set of modules and each module is assigned to an individual or team to write. When the modules are linked up and the system as a whole becomes operative, there is no single person who knows in detail how it works.

The modular approach is everywhere visible nowadays, whether in manufactured objects like cars or in non-material structures like computer software.

Marx and Engels observed the human consequences of the division of labour in the factories of Victorian Britain, where a workman might spend his entire working life turning out rivets without ever setting eye on the manufactures of which the rivets would form part. The alienation of the worker from the fruits of his labour, Marx and Engels said, leads to a kind of psychic indifference that infects all his relations with the world.

I wouldn't want to push too far the similarities between alienation – what you call feeling disconnected – and psychic regression. Nonetheless, the division of labour is fundamental to the modern economy, where most projects are too complex and extensive for a single pair of hands or, when it comes to intellectual work, too vast for a single intelligence to encompass in all their detail. Under such conditions, the work-experience of a group engaged in a modular job of work (a 'team') may be as alienated as that of an individual worker. Like the individual, the team can be working within a kind of blind cell, fulfilling instructions from above and cut off from fellow workers (I use the word 'fellow' with some qualms) in their own blind cells.

(3) How does one get to be a member of a group? Much of the time, it seems to me, one simply finds oneself belonging to a group, as opposed to freely and consciously choosing to join it. Thus one is *born into* a nation, a class, a caste, a race, a religion. At an early age one is sent to school where one joins a group of schoolmates one has never laid eyes on before. Even when, as an adult, one freely takes a job, one rarely knows beforehand who one's workmates will be. In these cases one can say that one is *thrown into* the group.

You suggest that a strongly felt membership of a group, a sense of belonging, need not be accompanied by regression in a psychological sense. I would put the emphasis elsewhere. I would say that involuntary group membership often results in regressive behaviour, as a way of blocking out an unhappy sense of not belonging yet not being able to get out. Such regression is like deliberately getting drunk to anaesthetise intolerable feelings.

Out of membership of great involuntary groups, like religion or caste or nation, one can, I have no doubt, get an enormous sense of security and validation and even pride. But belonging to an inescapable group can also be the root of a debilitating lifelong quarrel.

You sparked off our discussion of group regression by talking of your own experiences in the health service, and I responded with my experience as part of an audience listening to music. Let me hazard a thesis: that being part of a group constituted by a common focus (on a musical performance, a football game, a political leader or Führer, even a movie) is fundamentally different from being part of a group that is constituted from above to perform a task. In the first case the group is amorphous and vague in number; in the second case it is structured and specific in number. In the first case membership is a private matter: one can withdraw at any moment, without explanation. In the second case one contracts to enter the group and cannot withdraw without penalty. I could go on listing differences, but the claim I want to make is a simple one: that a psychological theory capacious enough to encompass both kinds of groups is likely to be vacuous. The kind of group that Le Bon and Freud had in mind was the first one, characterised by a dissolution of ego boundaries. The second kind of group, the kind you get in offices and schools and hospitals, seems to me more interesting and also more amenable to analysis.

My own group experience has been in classrooms rather than in hospitals; also in academic departments, whose fractious, childish tendencies have often been noted. What we call the problem of discipline in the school classroom is almost invariably a problem of handling regressive behaviour. It is not that some child or other is threatening to take over command of the group from the teacher (that is, slay the father). Rather, the problem is that order in the classroom is continually ('as soon as my back is turned') being infringed by preverbal, often obscene noises, aggressive or antisocial acts (surreptitious blows, hair-pulling, exhibitionism), wilful stupidity, and so forth. It is as if the children are regressing to an anarchic infancy; to get them to 'behave', that is to say, to 'act their age', requires a huge effort from the teacher, an effort that is beyond the psychic means of some. In the old days it often called forth, in the name of discipline, exhibitions of exemplary physical violence – regressive behaviour of another kind.

Regressive behaviour can persist throughout the years of schooling. It is not unknown among undergraduates at university. It is hard to make sense of it unless one conceives of it as a form of protest. Protest against what? At an individual level, against being plunged into an involuntary group; and at a group level, against having order imposed from above. That is to say, the child wants to be free, which means being able to choose, at a whim, whether to be alone or to be in a group; and also being free to choose which group to join.

We should not forget that, in its origins in nineteenth-century England, universal compulsory education was a form of incarceration under another name. Its stated objective was to fit every child in the country with the three Rs; but what it was also meant to achieve was to get children off the streets while their parents were at work.

The antithesis of the school class, the group constituted from above by the rational criteria of age, scholastic ability, and so forth, is the gang, the group that constitutes itself, from within, on grounds that are hard for the outsider to penetrate and may simply have to be called elective affinities.

At school there is pressure on each child to belong to a gang, big or small. The pressure comes from the inherited collective culture of children but also from obscure internal forces. The child who belongs to no gang is unhappy and is made to feel unhappy. I would guess that the psychology of the childhood gang is an even richer field of exploration than the psychology of the classroom.

∞

AK – The collective endeavour I had in mind was not a cathedral or a pyramid, but socialised medicine in the form of the NHS. In contrast to the slave workers you describe, NHS doctors and nurses have generally gone about their business with willing dedication. In many of the better services staff work together well to provide care for patients, feeling a sense of pride in their shared achievements.

I am afraid this is all changing. An inquiry into high death rates in the Mid-Staffordshire NHS Trust was published in early 2013.[10] It concludes that managers were so preoccupied with financial results and hitting external targets set by the government that basic patient care went out the window. The NHS is currently in the grip of the sort of alienation you describe: despite the rhetoric of care, government and NHS managers are working to one agenda, the agenda of profit and loss, and ground-level staff are working to another. We are currently a very unhappy and dysfunctional big group.

I most certainly think that a family is a group: a small group I grant you, but in its essence a group. But more importantly, at least for our purposes, I think the family is the place where we first learn or fail to learn about group life in the sense of relinquishing the exclusivity of a one-to-one relationship and being one of a number – or one in triangular relation to the relationships of others.

Of course what I am referring to here is the **Oedipal situation**, the story at the centre of Freudian psychology of the move from a two-person to a three-person relationship.

Before considering what this story might have to tell us about the way individuals relate to groups there is the important question of relevance to address for, as you rightly point out, it is not the majority of families in the world that consist of a neat triangle of mother, father and babe. (Although I would put it to you that there is universal significance in the fact that this is how we all begin, whatever happens afterwards. For all of us, the pairing of our mother and father, the so-called facts of life, holds a profound but forbidden fascination — a fascination that is so difficult to accommodate in our conscious mind that it is often expressed through a strange, unaccountable indifference or through repulsion, the insistence that this is something that cannot or must not be thought about or known.)

Psychoanalysts can get people's backs up by talking as if an outdated, outmoded model of the family were both the norm and the ideal, as if a particular and narrow form of conventional, middle-class family life is being universally prescribed in order to produce mentally healthy human beings. But in contemporary psychoanalytic thought Oedipal development is conceptualised in terms of stages in the way relationships are represented inside the mind, and not what goes on in concrete relationships with external figures.

What this means, jumping the gun for a moment, is that on the basis of the psychology of the situation the child of a single parent or a child in a large family might well achieve a level of reflective thinking about themselves in relation to others that the child in a small family with two parents does not. It is, once again, an internal and not an external matter.

To go back to the beginning of the Oedipal story, as retold by contemporary psychoanalysis: the first stage or scene in the theatre of the mind of the infant involves two objects, which is all that can be taken in at this point by the baby's small mind and body.

There is the infant self, not experienced for the first few months or so as a self but more as the source of need — need in the form of a feeling of hunger, a feeling of cold or of pain. And there is the Other, not thought about as another person at the beginning, but as objects and parts of objects that do or do not respond to need — the breast that satisfies, the breast that frustrates, the arms that provide warmth and holding, the arms that will not come. It takes a good few months, about six it is thought, for mental pictures of a self in relation to another whole person to emerge.

In Freudian psychology it is the self that exists from the beginning, then the self in relation to another (our first lesson in love and hate, in satisfaction and frustration). Then it is the self in relation to another who is in turn in relation to another (our first lesson in morality, in conducting ourselves to accommodate the needs and desires of others). In Kleinian psychology it is the self in relation to another from the start, even in the womb. Selfhood independent of relationships does not exist.

The integration of the different parts that make up the experience of the other into the form of another whole person heralds, as I described before, what Klein called 'the depressive position': a state of mind that can accommodate complexity and ambivalence. The Other, usually in the form of the mother, comes into fuller perspective for the developing infant as a person in their own right, someone who produces feelings of frustration, disappointment and longing, alongside feelings of love, calm and satisfaction.

The ability to see others as complex beings, capable of good, bad and the shades of grey in between, and to tolerate frustration and ambivalence is, it seems to me, essential for constructive engagement in group life. It is one of the things that begin to make it possible for people to come together to work, with time and effort, on a shared approach to a problem. Without this ability in some or many of the members of a group, collectives fall prey to them-and-us thinking, either breaking up into cliques or small groups within a group, or organising themselves around the perception of an external enemy.

An important point to be made here is that the developmental tasks associated with the depressive position are not seen as things we do once and for all and never go back to. We do not achieve the ability to bear complexity and ambiguity for good. Instead these tasks are conceptualised within psychoanalysis as themes that re-emerge throughout the life cycle, and most particularly at times of stress and development.

Nowadays we tend to think that the extent to which the work of integration is accomplished by the growing mind strongly affects its capacity to take in a third object in the form of the internal representation of a relationship between one's primary object and an Other – be they a parent's or carer's partner, a sibling, or an interest or activity. The assumption is that if the infant is secure in their primary relationship, if they are sure of their access to the person upon whom they are most fundamentally dependent, it is more possible to think of sharing them.

The ability to build a space in one's own mind for the relationships between others — for the independent existence of such relationships as a source of creativity over which one has limited control but which one can draw upon and rely on — also determines, in my view, the way one approaches work in a group. In a memorable paper Ronald Britton described this space for thinking as triangular, referring to the capacity to take up a third position in order to observe oneself in relation to another.[11] In this scheme, Oedipal development forms the basis for a particular type of reflective thought — a type of thought that is likely to be of particular significance to the extent to which group dynamics take a constructive or a regressive turn, since much of what we do in groups is to act or react in response to what is going on between other people.

To my mind, the ability to accommodate a third person in the mind in part determines the capacity to accommodate a fourth, fifth, sixth person and so on. Three stands for three and up.

The individual who cannot bear to be excluded from the relationships of others may adopt an authoritarian stance, seeking to control the activities of other people in a group and getting between others so that the only person they relate to in any meaningful way is the leader. We refer to this form of leadership when we talk of the principle of 'divide and rule'. Or they may withdraw from the group, denying their reliance upon it and taking themselves out of any possibility of triangular relationship. Or they may act within the group as if it were a series of two-person relationships, sharing secrets and conspiracies with other individuals and avoiding any sense of the group as a corporate body made up of a number of persons.

I could go on . . . But my main point is that each individual member of a group will have internalised early family experiences in ways that will be brought to bear upon the external group situation. These will determine the nature and level of their involvement in group life, what they demand and expect from others, at both a conscious and unconscious level, and the power for creativity or destructiveness called from within them by the group situation.

NINE

Group mentality in collectives not based on the family, such as juvenile gangs or armies. Melanie Klein on mother and child. The scientific status of accounts of early childhood experience. The role of sympathetic projection in understanding the experience of others. Sympathetic identifications as fictions; the fiction-like status of Kleinian theory. Engagement between human beings as engagements between fictions. The ideal of a therapeutic psychology prepared to work with fictions. Gangs and gang membership: personal experience. Aspects of the gang psyche not captured by a psychology of the individual.

The role of the Other in opening one to self-knowledge. I-and-you truth in the consulting room. The creative work of the parent in bringing up the child to make sense of experience. Donald Winnicott on the development of the false self. Real — as opposed to fiction-like — knowledge of the other. Projection as experienced in everyday social interactions. Projection in psychoanalytic theory. Projection within groups. Regression. Tolerant and less tolerant attitudes toward fantasy within the therapeutic profession in Britain. The orthodox position on symbolisation. Anne Alvarez on understanding the child's play from the inside.

❖

JMC – It barely needs mentioning that behind the outline you provide of how to think about early-life experience there lies a huge body of psychological literature. I know this literature only in the sketchiest of ways and at an amateurish level. But it has been our understanding from the beginning that an amateur and an outsider like myself may possibly have a contribution to make. So let me respond to the gist of what you say, and then venture a general comment on how I see the Kleinian account of Self (the infant self that is not yet a proper self) and Other.

Your main point is that what we learn from our experience of the Oedipal triangle will be fundamental to, indeed may even determine, our later success in working with groups. In this connection you are not afraid to use the u-word: your claim holds universally, you say. Thus you implicitly reject the notion I earlier floated: that the family does not have to be the model for the group, and therefore that to understand how groups work we may need a psychology that is not based on the family, in particular on the Oedipal triangle.

To anchor the discussion it may be a good idea to bring to the fore what you and I have in mind respectively when we speak about groups. Your example of a group (aside from the family group) is the National Health Service, or more specifically certain units within the NHS. Such a group is culturally and historically specific; how far one can generalise from it is open to question.

A group psychology worthy of the name – it seems to me – needs to account for a wider range of groups. A case in point would be the gang of boys or youths I mentioned in our last exchange, a group that does not relate in an obvious way to a family. An even more difficult example is provided by the army, or, if the entirety of an army is too large to be considered a group, by the constituent units of an army.

I call the army a difficult case because the army has its own ideas about developmental psychology and about the models of relating to others that new recruits bring with them from their family experience. Army training commences with a deliberate purging of all the recruit has learned about relationships with others, including seeing others as complex beings and tolerating ambivalence (I quote your words). I won't elaborate. Let me merely say that the goal of reforming the mind of the recruit is to produce an obedient soldier who will function well in a group.

You can object that the psychological reformation practised by armies amounts to no more than behavioural conditioning. But the fact is that, by its own definition of functioning, army training produces groups that function better than most other groups, including units of the NHS. A good theory of group psychology ought to have room for army-style groups with their own army-style psychology.

Let me go on to something quite different, Melanie Klein's account of early childhood experience.

Klein's account, like many psychological accounts, has an interesting double status. First, it is a scientific hypothesis no different in essence from hypotheses in natural science. We posit our hypothesis, then check it against the relevant data. As long as the data does not contradict the hypothesis the hypothesis is confirmed, or at least not disconfirmed. But second, since it is a hypothesis about human experience, we as human beings can and do have intuitions of our own as to its correctness. Unless we are rigorous positivists and insist on exploring human psychology in exactly the same way we would explore the psychology of rats, these intuitions play a substantial role in whether, at a lived level, we entertain (welcome) the hypothesis or not.

For instance, accounts of infant psychology often refer to the infant's *needs*. We don't find it necessary to give a scientific definition of need because on the basis of our own experience we can intuit what a need is, indeed even what it feels like. I call such intuitions *sympathetic* intuitions.

(I need hardly say that our intuitions are no reliable guide to the truth and may even have to be consciously put aside: think for instance of the world-picture offered by quantum physics, which for the most part runs counter to our intuitions.)

We have broached the subject of sympathy and sympathetic

identification before now. Broadly speaking, I see sympathy as an inborn faculty in human beings which may or may not grow, may or may not atrophy, may or may not be fostered; I also see it as capable of extending itself beyond fellow human beings to other forms of life.

Sympathetic identifications allow us to enter other lives and to live them from the inside. It goes without saying that the other lives we live at such times are not necessarily the true lives of the others to whom they belong. Even when the other life which we are (for the time being) living is not a real life but the kind of life we encounter when we read novels, it is not necessarily the true life of the other that we are living – witness the very different understandings different readers have of characters in novels.

I would contend that our sympathetic identifications have a fiction-like status, and that our sympathetic intuitions can be relied on only to yield fictional truths.

From this point onward I want to be very cautious in my reasoning, restricting my remarks to hypotheses about human psychology, in particular infant psychology.

What Melanie Klein has to say about very young children does not run counter to empirical data about the behaviour of babies. Therefore what she says has the status of a valid hypothesis – valid until disconfirmed. Nevertheless, part of the attractiveness of her account lies in its intuitive appeal. Thus you are able to write easily of an infant self without structure, as simply a site of hunger or cold or pain. You can also write of a breast that appears and disappears frustratingly, constituting the entirety of the world that is the non-'self'.

Where does your confidence come from? The answer, I would guess, is that you can imagine such an existence; you can project yourself sympathetically into it; you can, briefly, be such a baby. The identification is further strengthened by an awareness that the baby into whose life you are projecting yourself is or was you yourself. Though you cannot consciously remember being that baby, you must have been it (her).

I don't want to pick nits here, but the fact is, the sole access we have to past mental states of our own is through memory. *I remember how frightened I was. I remember how I used to love him.* But we can't remember what it was like to be a neonate, any more than we can remember what life was like in the womb. For some reason or other, God did not build such capacity into us. When we sympathetically inhabit our neonate selves, we are inhabiting a fiction.

Fictions are neither true nor false, in the normal sense of those words. There may be another sense in which they can be true or false, but that is not relevant here. For my purposes, it is enough to say that Klein's account of neonate experience is a fiction. You happen to think it is a true account, and I tend to agree. But it is nevertheless a fictional account, a story about what it is like to be a baby.

I relate our whole discussion to an essay by the philosopher Thomas Nagel that has acquired near scriptural status, called

'What is it like to be a bat?'[12] Nagel's crucial move is to distinguish between two forms of the question: *What would it be like for a human being to be a bat?* and *What is it like for a bat to be a bat?* In its first form, he says, the question is answerable; in the second form it is not.

I disagree with Nagel. I think that by a strenuous effort of sympathetic projection one can reach a flickering intuition of what it is like for a bat to be a bat. But this does not amount to the claim that one can have intuitions of what it is *really* like for a bat to be a bat. In Nagel's terms, the only true, real knowledge one can have of what it is like to be anyone or anything in the world is a form of knowledge of what it is like to be oneself. Other such knowledge may be true, but its truth is the truth of fictions. This includes knowledge of what it is like for a neonate to be a neonate.

∞

AK – You make a clear and compelling statement: the only thing one can really know the truth about is oneself. But as a therapist trying to help people who are in distress, it is simply not relevant whether something is truth or fiction in the philosophical terms you set out. We have been over this ground before. I am not a philosopher, I am a psychologist, and fretting about the exact nature of the Truth with a capital T is not going to meet the situation that faces me, which is that of a human being, usually in great distress and confusion, wanting sympathy and understanding.

What usually matters most to the person seeking help is the type of relationship available to them in the consulting room. And so a mix of truth and fiction, however unsatisfactory in philosophical terms, offered by somebody who is trying, with all the intelligence, sympathy and understanding of which they are capable, to imagine the situation of the other person from the inside out is worth far more than a pure and lonely truth. An I-and-you truth, a relational truth, is much more valuable than one more separate and more certain.

Let me elaborate. Perhaps from a philosophical point of view all we can really know about – or the only *means* by which we can know about anything – is ourselves. But what the psychoanalytic theory of human relations, a powerful one in my view, holds is that true self-knowledge is not something that can be achieved alone, that we rely upon others to know ourselves. What it also puts forward is a theory of how we depend upon others in the early stages of development to learn how to know.

What this means is that a newborn baby needs to be thought about by another in order to start to contemplate, and to get to know themself. They need words to be given to wordless experience, a frame to be put around raw, unmediated experience. So the act of creative imagination that a parent or carer undertakes in order to think about what it is like to be a baby, and what it is like to be this particular baby, contributes to the baby's earliest sense of the truth about themself. You see parents doing this creative work all the time, sitting with a baby and wondering what it is they are feeling, what it is that satisfies or irritates, making sense on the baby's behalf of a particular type of behaviour or response.

The assumption is that the more a person has had of this type of care the more able they will be in childhood and later life to set about knowing the truth about themself – and, by extension, the truth about others.

The psychoanalyst Donald Winnicott wrote extensively on the subject of authenticity.[13] He constructed the notion of the false self, which develops when the young child takes in too much of the truth of the other at the expense of their own emerging capacity to know about themself. The metaphor of force-feeding was used by Winnicott to describe the way that external nourishment, in this case of the symbolic kind, can be pushed upon the infant, or taken in by them wholesale, rather than sensitively supplied in response to their appetite for knowledge.

A current patient comes to mind whose most pressing problem is that she thinks continuously and compulsively about others, to the point where she really knows very little about herself. She can talk with authority about others, about their feelings, their motivations, and so on. But when it comes to thinking about herself she gets stuck. Her parents were intensely preoccupied with their own considerable troubles when she was small, and she had the feelings and the upsets of others to deal with rather than being helped to deal with her own. Her defence seems to have been to deny the existence of feelings and upsets in herself altogether; in her mind it is as if other people are real and she is not; other people have feelings that it is possible to know something about, she does not have them. In therapy I am working to help her build a sense of self, and she is understandably sensitive to the extent to which I impose my understanding upon her, and the extent to which I am able to attend properly to her.

It is true that much of the time when we are with others we have to work pretty hard, with strenuous effort as you put it, to understand what it is like to be them. But if the psychoanalytic theory of projection is to be believed, there is the potential for moments when we get a relatively undistorted sense of what it is like to be someone other than ourselves. Something is communicated to us unconsciously so that we are made to feel something on another's behalf – to get, if you like, a real, unadulterated taste of what it is like to be them. The idea is that people do this with unwanted aspects of the self, and that communication of this type is based both upon a desire not to know something about oneself and upon a genuine hope, however ambivalently held, for understanding.

The example I always use when I am teaching is that of the bully, the person who is quite adept at making others feel small and intimidated so that he or she does not have to feel this way himself or herself. Most people know this about bullies. But there are also people who make us feel clever or funny or boring or awkward, and it is always worth asking the question as to whether there is an aspect of our response that can best be understood as a projection: an aspect of the other that has been passed across to us for safekeeping, as it were, rather than as a more straight-forward communication from one person to another. There is the teacher, for example, whose talent for encouraging and promoting others is based on confidence in their own knowledge and ability; and there is the teacher whose same evident skill operates at the cost of, or directly out of, a bewildering lack of this same sense in themselves. They give to others what they cannot take ownership of on their own behalf.

Psychoanalytic theory proposes that we project into others those parts of ourselves which we want to get rid of, or not to know about, and so, in the terms of your argument, that we actively, if unconsciously, invite others to know something about us that we do not know about ourselves. As therapists we are taught to recognise this sort of communication by its alien quality, its otherness, by the fact that, for instance, at the start of the session one felt alert but one is now feeling dull or bored, or that one was quite calm but now experiences a sense of panic. In my experience it is often very helpful to pay attention to the precise details of this type of experience – helpful I mean, in learning something about the patient's state of mind.

Where this takes us in terms of our thinking about groups I am not sure. I certainly think that unconscious communication in the form of projection goes on a great deal in groups. Individuals or subgroups take up roles on behalf of others and find themselves behaving in ways that would be uncharacteristic of them outside the group. We often see a group situation, for example, in which authority becomes located in one person and disavowed by others; or one in which vulnerability and disturbance are located in one person, someone we call the scapegoat, so that others can maintain the illusion of being free of these uncomfortable feelings.

I understand a regressed group to be one in which a lot of this type of unconscious communication is occurring, but the group has very little awareness of it. So if we are thinking of a typically hierarchical arrangement in an army unit, for instance, a regressed or dysfunctional situation is one in which the people playing different roles feel compelled to do so even when there is no need. A more functional situation would be characterised by the same clearly demarcated roles, but underpinned by an understanding of why people are acting within the group in the way they are. From a psychological point of view there is nothing wrong with an army if an army is behaving like an army, organising itself in a sensible way to face a military situation; but there is a problem if the troops have given away so much of their authority that they cannot think when required to do so, or the commander becomes so power crazy that he does not know when he needs the help or advice of others.

∞

JMC – One.

I am troubled by a suspicion that I have been unfair to Melanie Klein, who is, I know, important to you. Furthermore, I ought to take to heart your reminder that a patient who comes to a therapist in distress wants sympathy and understanding, not a disquisition on the difference between fictional truths and fictional fictions.

But you press the point too far when you call the relation between patient and therapist, a relation based on the therapist's human sympathy as well as her professional insight, a 'relational truth'. This makes the concept of truth so wide as to evacuate it of usefulness. I would prefer to say that patient and therapist feel the relationship to be authentic, thereby leaving open the question of whether the engagement might not be between two constructions, the patient's and the therapist's.

My preference for leaving the question open is not meant in a spirit of destructive scepticism. I think we can entertain the notion that we are continually engaging with constructions (fictions) of others, rather than with their 'real' selves, without feeling we are at the edge of an abyss. We can also entertain the more plausible (and more interesting) notion that our engagements are with a constantly changing interplay between shadows (fictions) and glimpses of the real.

The point I want to make is that any close or intimate relation with another person is likely to involve sympathetic projections, even when the relation is between a patient and a therapist. Thus I would be in favour of a therapeutic psychology which, instead of trying to get beyond or through such projections or fictions, treating them as though they necessarily hide the truth, could instead easily and openly accept our fictionalising of self and others as part of life.

Here is a simple example of what I mean by accepting fictions as part of life. With particular reference to the young child (though it probably holds for us throughout our lives), you write: 'We rely upon others to know ourselves.' What if we were to translate that claim as follows: 'We need the fictions of others about us in order to form our fictions of ourselves'?

Here is a more challenging example. You write: 'The more a person has had of this type of [sympathetic] care the more able they will be . . . to set about knowing the truth about themselves.' Translation: 'The more a person has been offered sympathetic fictions of herself, the more easily she will be able to live within the fiction(s) she holds of herself.'

Two.

I have written of my interest in what we are loosely calling group psychology, but I continue to struggle to say anything constructive about it. I have looked at Bion's *Experiences in Groups*, but got nothing from it. I hold onto Menzies Lyth's insight that almost as soon as a group forms a regression seems to take place, and therefore that if a group wants to prosper it must somehow confront the challenge (one might even want to say, the allure) of regressing; but I don't know where to take this insight.

I have looked again at Gustave Le Bon *(Psychology of Crowds)* and have confirmed my impression that there is nothing there worth building on except for the intuition, which I share, that the psychology of the group is unlike the psychology of the individual.

I still feel that youthful gangs will have more to tell us about group psychology than the rather artificial groups Bion worked with – groups of people tasked with reflecting on what it is like to be in a group – or the occupational groups we find in Menzies Lyth.

My guess is that a proper psychology of groups will emerge not from our tradition, which had its birth in the hothouse domestic environment of the Viennese Jewish intelligentsia, but from some unsuspected part of the world where group life is the norm and the concept of the family is looser and/or wider than ours – Asia or Africa, perhaps.

My mind keeps going back to the most ganglike gang I ever belonged to, when I was eight years old. There must have been five or six of us in the gang. After school we used to roam the quiet streets of Rosebank looking for things to do. Once we stood at the front gate of a beautiful double-storeyed residence and shouted and screamed and rattled the letterbox in the hope that someone would emerge – ideally some grown-up in a state of puzzled consternation – at which point we would run off, laughing. On another occasion we lobbed pebbles through the open window of someone's house, scores of pebbles, perhaps hundreds – they must have made a terrible mess.

Why did we behave in this way? Committed by small boys, such acts are usually dismissed as 'mischief', as 'getting up to mischief'. One is supposed to find acts of childish mischief tiresome yet loveable: not to find them loveable brands one as a sourpuss. Yet it was the ambition of those boys *not* to be recuperated as loveable. The so-called mischief we carried out was not mischievously intended. Our actions, silly and ineffectual as they were, were aimed at creating enemies or victims (in this case the two cannot be distinguished) whose outrage could then be ridiculed and who in the future could be subjected to further attacks. The *raison d'être* of the gang, I would suggest, is to have enemy-victims who can be attacked in the name of defending the gang. A gang without enemies is inconceivable.

Of course we weren't the first children to form a gang and do antisocial things. We got the idea from tradition, the traditional culture of boys. Every aspect of our behaviour can be captured by the notion of Oedipal revolt – every aspect save one: group identity, in this case, gang identity. If I think back carefully to what happened when the gang assembled of an afternoon, it seems to me that we came together as ourselves, as individuals, in our social identities; but then at a certain moment someone said, 'Are we all here?' after which we dropped our real-life identities and became gang members with the made-up identities we were embracing that particular day, bank robbers or outlaws or whatever. We assumed these fictional identities and we confirmed each other in these identities, and thus a group fiction came into being which sustained us through the afternoon.

I cling to the belief that there is something to be learned from gangs like that – from the way in which the group slips into a paranoid mode in which aggression is rationalised as self-defence, but also from the ease with which children can come together and give themselves to a communal gang fiction ('fantasy'), which they then inhabit for what feels to them the right length of time before they emerge from it and return to their real lives, keeping the fiction in reserve for another after-noon.

∞

AK – If psychoanalysts do not accept fiction, fantasy and make-believe as an ordinary, healthy part of life, then I really do not know who does. But perhaps what you are reacting to is a certain attitude towards fiction, or its day-to-day manifestations in play, dream and fantasy: an attitude that I would characterise as disap-proving and puritanical, and that implicitly invokes a relationship between fiction and reality in which fiction is the inferior party and should always be relinquished in favour of an engagement with reality.

Psychotherapists vary, I am sure, in the way in which they treat such products of the imagination, as to whether they approach a patient's fantasy with open interest, or are disturbed by it and feel the need to shut exploration down. I am reminded of the visitor to an art gallery who cannot respond with curiosity to the pictures in front of them because they are too busy worrying about not understanding things. The panicky, anxious thought is this: 'I don't know WHAT this could possibly mean.' Or: 'This obviously means that, no further questions please.'

From a clinical point of view it is interesting to think about the various types of symbolic or symbolising activity that map onto different stages of human development and serve different psychological purposes. I will try and state the contemporary British psychoanalytic position on this in very broad terms – or at least one iteration of it. I will rely on a recent chapter on the development of play and the imagination written by an experienced and well-respected child psychotherapist called Anne Alvarez.[14]

Alvarez works with extremely disturbed and deprived children, in whom the ability to play and to symbolise is constitutionally thwarted or very delayed. Unlike most of us she has spent a lot of time with children who cannot play, and she has observed first-hand how the failure to symbolise goes hand in hand with cut-off, affectless states of mind and what she describes as a disturbing failure of interest in the contents of the human mind and the possibility of meaning. There is often in these children a sticky, ritualistic attachment to the concrete, object world, as if in the absence of a symbolic picture of the self in relation to what is outside of it the physical world must be clung to all the more tightly. It is not that without symbolisation to get in the way there is a more direct or improved relation to reality. Instead there is a different type of connection between inside and outside, one that has to function without the help of representation to build links between things and across space and time.

In general terms Alvarez sees as outdated the idea that play is somehow opposed to the reality principle and that we need as therapists to use our interpretations to get behind play to understand what is really going on. She invokes Freud's account of his grandson playing the cotton-reel game to articulate different ways in which the same game can be played, depending on the state of mind and stage of development of the child.

Freud described how his grandson played with a cotton reel in his mother's absence. The child repeatedly let the cotton out and drew it back again, exclaiming '*fort*' or 'gone' as he let it out, and '*da*' or 'there' as he reeled it back in again. Freud saw in the little boy's play the enactment of a small drama of loss and recovery carried out in response to his mother's absence. There is the first possibility that the child played the game in order to simply escape a difficult situation, pretending to himself that absences and reunions are something he could bring about himself and control. This is symbolisation that is inferior to reality, in the sense that it operates as a poor substitute for what we do not actually have. The symbolic qualities of the cotton reel are not being used, at least not in a creative way, because it functions at this point as no more or less than a stand-in: it is taken in the mind for the thing itself. When therapists work on the assumption that a fantasy or daydream is nothing more than an escape from an aspect of reality that is difficult or unbearable, they are invoking a similar model of the relationship between the real and the symbolic.

An alternative is that the little boy used the game, at least in part, as a more or less conscious attempt to gain mastery over the feelings he had in response to being left. 'I will lose you and I will find you,' he says to himself, as he casts out the reel and brings it back in again. He turns an experience of powerlessness and vulnerability into one in which he is in charge of comings and goings. But the emphasis here is on the fact that he primarily does this, not in order to deny what is going on, but in order to begin to cope with it: in order to start to become a child who can face up to such things. This interpretation of events owes a great deal to Donald Winnicott, for whom imagination was integral to the whole business of taking things in and making experience our own so that we can, in mental terms, begin to do something with it.

But as Alvarez reminds us, there is another important possibility. There could be a child who plays the cotton-reel game at what we might think of as a higher symbolic level in order to explore 'the properties' of the absent mother and of absent objects in general, and the nature of his or her relationship to them. This, of course, is art: the use of symbols to explore and to understand experience.

After all, how do I really know what I think about this person or thing and my relationship to them or it if all I do is react to them or it in the world? It is partly a question of distance and perspective. I need to draw back and create some distance to think about the object, to conjure it up symbolically in my mind, to think metaphorically about what it is and is not like and to gain a better sense of the object and what it means to me.

I think all of us can demonstrate this attitude of intolerance towards fantasy and make-believe. Recently I facilitated what we call a Reflective Practice Seminar, in which a group of clinical psychology trainees hear in detail about a case and share ideas about how to make sense of complex clinical material. A trainee told us about a man in his late forties, someone who seemed outgoing and competent and held down a good job; but he was living with his parents, having frequent fights with his mother, and was also suffering from severe obsessional-compulsive symptoms. He had to have all sorts of things kept in exactly the right place at home and spent hours each day cleaning.

The feature of the case which concerns me in relation to our exchange is this: we were told that this man had collected a large number of ornaments with an idea that they would be displayed in the home that he would move into and live in independently one day. He spent time regularly cleaning these ornaments, keeping them carefully bagged up and getting furious with his mother if she touched or moved them.

Now at first the bags of ornaments were described by our seminar group as a symptom of the man's disorder. He was clearly 'a hoarder'. This fantasy of a home of his own was an escape, preventing him from facing up to *his* problems. We, like his parents, felt impatient with his silliness and lack of realism. But we began to wonder – and the resources of the group, of a number of minds working together on a problem, helped enormously with this. We wondered about his fantasies of a life of his own, as he bought the ornaments and cleaned then. We thought about the value of showing an interest in the ornaments and what they meant so as to better understand – or rather to begin to understand – what he wanted in life. We thought how hopeful it was that he was dreaming of a bright, beautiful life that was different to the difficult, very bleak situation he was in, and how this could be integrated into the therapeutic work he was doing to help him move forwards in his life.

TEN

Doubts about a therapy that aims to guide the patient to greater awareness of the full reality of other people. Are our interactions 'real' or are they interactions between projected, fictive selves? Teaching young children to reason. The importance of fantasy to the child. The school classroom and the question of discipline. Forms of resistance to learning in the tertiary-level classroom. Uses of psychoanalysis in understanding resistance. A caveat about amateur psychoanalysis. Gangs of young men. The feeling-world of the gang.

The traditional classroom and its physical set-up. Kinds of learning that are inhibited by this set-up. Feelings of curiosity and the anxieties that accompany curiosity; feelings between students and teachers. How the group situation suppresses conscious awareness of such feelings. Large groups (crowds) versus small groups: differences in group dynamics. Channelling the psychic energy of the group in the interest of progress and learning. Transference in the classroom. How the teacher can profit by being aware of the transference. Transference and

counter-transference in the therapeutic setting. Transference as
a mode of symbolic thinking. The need for creative analysis of
symbolic thought as expressed in transference.

❖

JMC – On the subject of the therapeutic dialogue, I think I am
getting a clearer picture of where we agree and where we disagree.
In respect of our disagreements, I have a clearer idea of which
are negotiable and which are firmly rooted.

Let me try to spell out what I see as our fundamental difference. You can then let me know if I am travestying you.

In my reading of you, you would like to help your patient – the
dialogical 'you' to your 'I' – to live a more self-aware, more productive, happier life, where happy takes on the full range of connotations
it has in the rich history of happiness in Western thought. Part of
living a more self-aware life is understanding what your real relations are with other people. This means, on the one hand, having
some appreciation of the fullness of the lives these other people lead
(they are not just phantoms who vanish into the air when you cease
to think about them) and of the place you realistically occupy in
their lives; on the other hand, understanding what it is you want or
need from them (what your interest is in them).

My position is more sceptical. Specifically, I have doubts about
how deep the appreciation and the understanding can extend that
you would like to foster in the patient. I feel that, seen from the

outside, the lives of other people almost always have a somewhat made-up, fictional quality. The capacity (which I think of as a moral capacity) to project oneself sympathetically into someone else's life is rare, the capacity for sustained sympathetic projection even rarer. None of this amounts to a novel claim. But, more radically, I feel that our own needs and desires have a similar fiction-like status. We attribute them to ourselves. We try them out and if they suit us we inhabit them. A desire that is too thoroughly understood loses its force and in effect ceases to be desire.

Hence all my talk about relations between people as a matter of interlocking fictions. When the fictions interlock well, the relation works or seems to work (I am not sure that there is a difference between the two). When they don't interlock, conflict or disengagement follow.

All of the above by way of summary.

There is something interesting to be said along such lines about why people who have been erotically engaged with each other gradually become disengaged – some analysis of what happens to desire when the fiction one holds about the other becomes too stable, too dependable. But that would take us off course.

There is also something to be said about relations between people and animals, particularly pet animals. Animals do nothing to discourage the wildest fantasising on our part about what they are thinking or feeling. What we are engaging with in the case of an animal – the animal's 'personality' – is a fiction of our own creation. It cannot be otherwise. As for whether animals have corresponding fictions of us, that will forever be unknown, since we have no idea what it means or even feels like for an animal to entertain a fiction.

I notice that you have nothing further to say about groups – that is, about the two examples of groups I wrote about, childhood gangs and schoolroom classes. Though I must confess I have no suggestions for how to theorise the psychology of such groups, I don't want to abandon the topic. I hope we can return to it later.

Speaking of classes, I recently watched a documentary film called *Ce n'est qu'un début,* released in 2010. The film records several sessions of a course in philosophy (more accurately, in philosophising) run by a French schoolteacher. The interesting thing about the course is that the students are pre-schoolers.

As the sessions progress, some of the students lose interest and fall behind, but a substantial number catch on to what it means to discourse philosophically, and thrive. By the end they are talking in a way that any intelligent adult would appreciate: they know what it means to propose a thesis and buttress it with an argument, they know what it means to adduce evidence.

Two things struck me about the film, and the project behind it. One is that reasoned discourse can be taught, and to a receptive child can be taught fairly rapidly. The other is that once a child is able to discourse reasonably, the need for symbolic play is (I hypothesise) reduced. I make this observation with Anne Alvarez and other developmental psychologists in mind, who argue for the vital importance of symbolic play.

How I feel about replacing play with discourse I am not sure. On the one hand, it is an admirable enterprise (and a very French one!) to teach reasoning to small, malleable minds. If Socrates were to pay us a visit from the Elysian Fields (les Champs-Élysées) he would, I am sure, smile and nod. We are born with the framework of a conceptual system within us, he would say; it merely takes a skilful interlocutor to draw ideas out of us and show us how to set them in motion. On the other hand, as you know, I am attached to the notion of fantasy, including play-fantasy. I would be sorry to see bright young souls turned into exemplary reasoning machines.

I remember at the age of eight or nine becoming aware of myself as a child inordinately given to fantasy. At the time I felt this to be a form of self-indulgence, and felt guilty about it; my feelings of guiltiness were fortified by the very puritan culture in which I lived, as well as by disapproving comments from people who knew me well, my uncles in particular (but not my mother). I compared myself with other children of my age, contrasting the ease with which they handled the real world with my own ineptitude. Nonetheless, I never thought of giving up my fantasy life and attaching myself to the real. Rather, I accepted fantasising as a kind of affliction that had been visited on me at birth, a congenital disease that I was doomed to carry.

I am glad, looking back, that I had the good sense not to cure myself of my disease. I hope those sweet little French children don't get the idea into their heads that rational analysis and reason-backed strategising is the only way there is of dealing with the world.

AK – A while ago, in discussing the psychology of groups, you wrote about your experiences as a teacher and about the problem of keeping discipline in the classroom. Let me give concrete form to the traditional pedagogical model by conjuring up the familiar image of the classroom of our schooldays. The blackboard (or whiteboard as it is now) and the teacher's big desk or table are at the front; there is a space there too where the teacher can walk about and talk to pupils. The pupils' smaller desks are arranged in a number of vertical rows, and the pupils at the back are more able to get away with talking or daydreaming or some other distracting activity. The ones who need to have an eye kept on them are usually put at the front.

The teacher in this scene is centre stage and his or her performance is aimed at imparting knowledge and understanding to the pupils or students; whereas the students' role, like so many proverbial empty vessels, is to receive knowledge and understanding. And, as you describe, the desks in this type of classroom are arranged in order to position the students in a series of separate, dyadic relationships with the teacher (the students at the back can't see the ones at the front and vice versa). It is also, perhaps more importantly, to inhibit their ability to form relationships with each other – or at least to limit and constrain the interactions that might potentially ensue between a group of lively, young students.

I have watched so many film scenes set in this type of classroom, usually in an American high school, in which the communications between students – who are of course more interested in each other than in anything else – are covert or subterfugal or outright rebellious. Paper notes are scrunched up and thrown or surreptitiously passed amongst students, amorous or aggressive comments are given in looks or hissed asides, texts are sent on mobile phones kept below the teacher's line of sight. The traditional classroom arrangement not only ensures – or attempts to ensure – that the most important relationships in the room are between each individual student and the teacher and operate with a degree of formality and distance. It also functions to prevent or at least to circumscribe the development of relationships between students in a way that could potentially be creatively linked with academic discussions in class. Such relationships can of course develop freely outside class – but that is a different matter.

I have an image for a moment of pupils at their desks as blinkered horses, blinkered of course because if the pupil/horse were able to look around freely at whatever interested or distracted them he or she would not obey orders and proceed in a straightforward fashion from A to B.

We all know that a good teacher has to have discipline and that without it children are not able to learn. The traditional classroom arrangement exists in order to regulate the stimulation and interest that are naturally present in a group of people meeting together with a teacher to discover and explore ideas. But I do wonder if there is a problem with such a set-up of allowing too little room for the expression and the development of natural, uninhibited curiosity – in one another as well as in the ideas that form the focus of the lesson – and thus of preventing links from being made between the material being taught and the real and more spontaneous life of the group.

This is an observation worthy of our attention, I think, because children and young people, especially teenagers, are so interested in themselves and one another; there are so many things that they really want to learn about that could be dismissed in the classroom context as personal and irrelevant, and what I am keen to open to question is the idea that the learning they are meant to be doing in the classroom would suffer if they were also able to explore some of their immediate concerns and preoccupations.

Ideally a course in a subject like literature or philosophy offers students the opportunity to explore the ideas of those who have thought in different and more profound ways about how to live in this world of ours, as individuals and in relationships with others, in a way that connects with the passions and preoccupations inside their heads.

What are some of the feelings which underlie the teaching or learning situation, in its most general sense and as we have all experienced it – both as children and as adults? There is, I would say, the primitive instinct of curiosity, the urge in all of us for exploration and adventure, which needs to be released to promote learning but is all too often inhibited and over-controlled. I would distinguish curiosity from other related feelings, among them the longing for knowledge and the desire for mastery, both of which emanate from a later stage of development.

These feelings are accompanied, I think, by strong anxieties. There is the fear about where curiosity will lead, about whether it will fuel a creative outcome or a messy and destructive one. There are anxieties about not having mastery and control, about powerlessness, and about being and remaining – for want of better words – stupid and inept. This is summed up with the question: How will I *ever* learn how to do X or Y?

There are other important feelings that are present in groups that meet to learn, even if they are largely unconscious, which have more to do with relationships between people. There is the desire to possess what the other has got, whether this is the students' desire for the superior knowledge and experience of the teacher, or the teacher's desire for the youthful potential of the students. This can take on the more positive forms of admiration and appreciation or the more negative aspect of envy. These feelings in turn create their own powerful anxieties, whether these involve individuals seeing themselves as small and inferior in comparison to others, feeling hopelessly diminished and discouraged, or whether they are a response to the hatred and aggression generated by envy.

What we can say is that these feelings are very likely to be present at some level in a group-learning situation, but may well not be part of the conscious experience of the group because the group or learning institution has organised itself without knowing it in this way so as to make sure that such feelings – at least the more threatening ones – are kept entirely at bay. They have literally been organised out of existence.

But the task of a group (consisting of teachers and students) that meets together to learn is surely to try as best as possible to manage and contain these feelings in the interests of the development of the students, rather than to simply repress them or organise them out of existence. It is admittedly a formidable task.

In relation to general group processes I will state the obvious: that groups are inherently very stimulating and exciting and threatening (I am referring now to the sense of internal threat provoked in the individual by the group situation); that large groups are stimulating and frightening in different ways from small groups, and that all groups; large or small, have to find some way of balancing the positive, life-promoting resources of the group with feelings that are genuinely more destructive and unhelpful. It is easy for a group to be, as it were, metaphorically flooded with affect, and for members to feel strongly pressured into getting rid of this discomfort – particularly when a group first meets and has no system in place for doing or thinking about anything. What we often see are groups that go one way or the other, that are lifeless and work at organising feeling out of existence (the work meeting) or that give members too much room for unbridled feeling (the gang). Perhaps if we lived in a society which laid more value on collective endeavour, we would have more experiences of lively, constructive group life. These experiences exist, for sure, but they are not easy to find.

৹৹

JMC – In the traditional classroom set-up, as you say, desks are ordered in rows to orient the student toward the front under the teacher's all-seeing eye, making any lateral transactions between students irregular. This set-up is quite naturally regarded by young children as a restriction on their freedom, and quite naturally they set about subverting it. While the theory is that the only transactions in the classroom that matter are those between teacher and students, so that all relations can be ignored except for the twenty or thirty teacher–student dyads, we all know that the room is in fact alive with interactions between students, that glances, whispers and gestures are continually passing between them. The best that the teacher can hope for is that, against this background buzz of communication, intermittent moments of actual learning can take place.

You are right to point out that maintaining discipline is a prerequisite for teaching and learning. What you don't mention is that maintaining discipline makes up an inordinately large part of the teacher's job, and that pitting oneself day after day against children, with their inexhaustible capacity to be naughty, can be exhausting and depressing and ultimately soul-destroying. Much though one might like to redeem naughtiness by claiming some kind of creative energy for it, the truth is that naughtiness is inimical to learning because it is so regressive. The teacher wants to take the class forward, to make the children grow; but the children, as a group, want to take the class backward to the anarchy of the nursery. Against the order and discipline that the teacher wants to institute, the children pit their burps and farts and giggles. There can be no clearer living illustration of the regressive tendencies of the group than the behaviour of a class of ten-year-old boys, once they get hold of the reins.

Why should this be so? Why should the discussion of the practice of teaching all too often devolve into a discussion of control of the classroom; and why should the power to create and maintain discipline all too often devolve into a mystique of personality: to maintain discipline what is needed in the teacher is a strong personality? Why, in the professional literature, is there so little psychological or indeed political analysis of what goes on in the classroom? (I say political because the task facing the teacher from the first day is that of establishing his/her authority; while for at least some of the children the great if unarticulated task is that of subverting an authority whose legitimacy is not obvious to them.)

My own experience as a teacher was mainly in the tertiary sector, and a university seminar is, I concede, quite unlike a primary-school classroom. Students behave more or less courteously. They give or appear to give the teacher their undivided attention. They seem to have put the old naughtiness behind them. What has become of the fount of naughtiness that in these same students' youthful selves seemed inexhaustible? Has naughtiness been outgrown, sloughed off, left behind? Perhaps. But when I cast my eyes over the seminar room a less encouraging explanation occurs to me. The naughtiest children are simply not here. The ones who have made it to the tertiary level are the sober ones, the ones who accept authority easily, who have not found it hard to adapt to the system. The naughty ones are elsewhere, creating a different kind of life for themselves.

We make it easier for ourselves to teach by removing the problem cases from the pool, leaving ourselves with the 'good' students, the students who don't 'have a problem' with authority, who have repressed their naughtiness for the sake of their own advancement. In a broader sense, the students who are left are those whom the system (and more broadly the culture) has selected in order to carry itself further.

Repression is the price we pay for progress or advancement. But there is a good repression and a not-so-good repression. The not-so-good repression is blind: we give up something without asking what it will cost us, and then shut our eyes to the question that continues to hover in the air: What did we lose to gain what we have gained?

Looking back on my own career as a university teacher, I am nagged by a feeling that in the classroom there were resistances at work which I tried to ignore or dismiss when I should instead have been trying to understand and counter them.

What was the nature of these resistances and how had they come into existence? One appealing explanation is that they were a residue left behind from the thousands of hours that students had spent in classrooms from the day they began their schooling, hours infused with boredom, resentment, and impatience. Entering the picture late in their schooling, I was having to bear the weight of my predecessors' failures.

But this explanation holds little water. The students who faced me on the first day of a typical semester were not bored or resentful or impatient. On the contrary, they were cheery, full of hope, determined to do their best. Whatever the resistances were that would emerge, the history these students brought with them was not one of sullen serfdom under domineering masters.

Whom should I have consulted, what should I have read if I had wanted to find out what was going on under the surface? Would psychoanalysis have helped? Would I have become a more successful teacher if I had reconceived of my role in the classroom as that of a therapist, bringing to the surface and exorcising the bad forces that were holding back our educational enterprise?

I don't think so. The relation of teacher to students is only tenuously like that of therapist to patient. Teacher and therapist are both trying to foster some kind of human growth, but few teachers have the training or the competence to fulfil a therapeutic as well as a pedagogical role. I certainly had neither. Furthermore, few therapists think of themselves as teachers — for one thing, they don't come into the room, the theatre of engagement, with a body of material that they want to transmit.

Let me fill out what I mean by tensions and resistances in the classroom by offering two instances.

One. It is fundamental to learning at all levels, but particularly in the academy, that one should be prepared to accept criticism and learn from it. In relation to the student, the teacher acts as both guide and critic: as guide, the teacher asks the student to take on new, challenging tasks; as critic, the teacher assesses the student's work and offers constructive commentary. In the humanities, where teachers spend a great deal of time reading and commenting on their students' written work, the critical role is central.

It is an everyday complaint among teachers that students pay too little attention to commentary. Students (the complaint goes) absorb the teacher's verdict on their work (the mark, the grade) but skip over suggestions for how to improve it. As a consequence the same old errors get repeated again and again, in essay after essay: from the same old spelling mistakes to the same old flawed discursive strategies. There is no progress; no learning takes place.

By refusing to accept, absorb, and act upon criticism, the student in effect refuses to learn. The teacher may have conscientiously fulfilled their side of the contract, but if the student evades fulfilling theirs, the transaction remains incomplete. The teacher may require the student to rewrite the essay; but if rewriting is conceived of as a punishment and performed grudgingly, what does it achieve for the student? Meanwhile the teacher remains in the dark about the source of the student's insistence on repeating and reinforcing old errors, their stubborn resistance to criticism, their refusal to accept the teacher's critical authority.

My sense of what is going on in such cases is that the student has split the teacher in two. On the one side the teacher is the embodiment of institutional authority, whose verdict, Yes or No, one must accept because one is not in a position to reject it. On the other side the teacher is a pretender who has not proved themself yet puts themself forward as a trustworthy guide. If you will follow me, the pretender says, I will lead you, educate you. The student replies: I am ready to do what the system demands – write the assignments and sit the examinations – in order to get the degree or diploma I desire, but why should I entrust myself to you? I refuse; or if refusing turns out to cost too much, I will go through the motions of obeying while in my dark core I continue to resist and refuse you.

The teacher who believes that by the act of enrolling for a course a student has acknowledged the educational authority of the teacher is as naive as the therapist who believes that by the act of entering therapy a patient has acknowledged the therapeutic authority of the therapist. The experienced therapist expects resistance in all kinds of disguised forms; the teacher should expect much the same. The advantage held by the therapist is that he or she is able to make of the patient's resistance the matter and substance of the therapy; whereas the teacher, even if he or she has the competence to engage directly with the individual student's resistance, does not have the time to respond to the range of individual resistances across the class while at the same time performing the role of transmitter of knowledge.

I need hardly spell out that in turning the teacher into an engulfing figure whose words of criticism – words which arrive with the weight of the institution behind them – threaten the integrity of the self, that is to say, the self he or she has self-constructed, the student is drawing the teacher into a transference whose manifestations – typically indirect – may nonplus or bewilder the teacher.

Two. My second instance involves equally puzzling behaviour on the part of the student, but of a different kind. Instead of resisting, the student follows the teacher slavishly, imitating their way of approaching the subject – what one might call their intellectual style – and even their mannerisms. This is done not as mockery but in what the student thinks of as a spirit of discipleship.

Such identification may be flattering to the teacher but it is hardly good for the student. The teacher certainly wants to be followed but also wants to encounter what we can call a healthy resistance along the road. No proper educational experience takes place if the student simply lets themself be invaded and taken over by the teacher – or rather, by their fantasy of who the teacher is, what the teacher stands for.

The kind of relationship I describe here must be all too familiar to the therapist. How one deals with it in therapy I don't know. It is certainly hard to deal with in teaching. How do you explain to the student that what you ultimately want for them is to achieve intellectual independence, and therefore that you want them to identify with you in this desire of yours for them to separate from you?

I should add that in my experience the student who slavishly imitates a teacher can be extremely fickle, turning against the revered figure with no apparent provocation (again this must be behaviour familiar in therapy). Sudden hostility often presents itself as a dawning realisation on the student's part of having been hoodwinked: that while being asked to 'be yourself' (express an independent view, be true to your own feelings and responses), the student is allowed to 'be yourself' only within certain limits, namely the limits of what the teacher finds acceptable. This accusation is extremely hard to defend against, since there is a kernel of truth to it.

The cases I have described – the first, where the student refuses to accept the teacher's authority; the second, where the student identifies closely with a fantasy of the teacher – are two extremes. But for the teacher to ignore such extremes and concentrate on less conflicted students in the middle seems to me a bad mistake. In fact I would go so far as to say in the case of the seemingly untroubled middle-of-the-road students who have easy relations with their teacher-figures, no real education is taking place. There has to be some level of resistance; and that resistance has to be worked through, so that, emerging at the other end, the student can look back and understand what they have been through.

The teacher has to be resisted, followed, resisted and followed, transcended, and left behind.

I don't want to stray too far from our central concerns, but I cannot resist pointing out that a working-through of the student's relation to the teacher figure cannot take place when the teacher is an image on a screen. Education is dialogical. Universities that do away with the old model of face-to-face instruction and replace it with canned (recorded) teaching are making a profound pedagogical error.

Leaving the classroom behind, let me make one last comment on the subject of gangs, and in particular gangs of young men behaving antisocially.

If you decide that you are going to live within the law, then you have to give up some of your desires. Giving up desires is not necessarily good for the individual, however much of a relief it may be to the collective.

It is a blessing to live in a peaceful, orderly society. But for some people the price of peace and order is too high: they have to give up too much of themselves, or what they feel to be themselves.

Societies have always had trouble with their cohort of young men, and conversely the cohort of young men have found themselves at odds with society. We should not divest ourselves of sympathy or fellow feeling for these young men. However unlikeable they may be as a group, their existential position is not enviable. In most societies, non-human as well as human, there is no need for large numbers of immature males. In the darkest view of things, war exists as a social institution so that young males can kill each other off.

There may be something to be gained by comparing gangs to wolf packs. I make this suggestion with due tentativeness – I don't want to seem to claim that the human gang is some kind of evolutionary throwback. But a lone wolf is a fish out of water.

Wolves, fish and many other animals become interesting from a psychological point of view only in groups. Isolated, turned into individuals, with an individual psychology attributed to them, there is not much to say about them.

If, instead of standing outside the gang and the feeling-world of the gang, we could somehow project ourselves sympathetically into that feeling-world at the same time that we try to understand how the psychic logic of the gang works, then perhaps we might come up with the beginnings of what at present seems unimaginable: a psychology of the group that itself manifests group-psychological processes.

∞

AK – Your description of the intense, changeable feelings projected onto the person of the teacher does indeed reflect the transference, the means by which the passionate libidinal attachments of early life are directed onto a figure in the present. Of course, transference reactions do not just take place in the consulting room; they are a feature of everyday life. But it is in the clinical situation that the therapist has permission to name these unconscious responses and to work to understand them. It's important to make the point that it isn't right to interpret transference reactions without explicit permission to do so – the permission granted by, for example, a patient's consent to undertake psychoanalytic psychotherapy.

In situations other than psychotherapy one can work in a way that is informed by an understanding of transference reactions, rather than making direct use of them. In broad terms such an application to the teaching situation might involve: (1) identifying for oneself the nature of the transference by developing understanding of what one represents for a particular student or class of students; (2) making sure that one does not just go along with this representation – either by fitting in with it or reacting against it; (3) where possible adjusting one's own behaviour in the situation to foster a relationship more in keeping with the learning task.

Your experience of university teaching parallels that of Freud in the therapy setting. He initially considered patients' strong, personal reactions, which in the early days tended to be expressions by female patients of romantic longing for male therapists, to be a thoroughly irritating obstacle to therapeutic work. But he was gradually convinced that they were integral to real learning – certainly in the interpersonal sphere. Indeed, in psychoanalytic psychotherapy if a transference reaction does not show itself (arguably it is always there, even if hidden), one cannot do the work. The psychoanalytic community followed a similar trajectory in their understanding of counter-transference responses (the emotional reactions of the therapist to the patient). Freud and Klein both regarded the counter-transference as something that got in the way of proper analytic work and should be dealt with separately by means of a personal training analysis. Then in 1952 Paula Heimann wrote a brave, inspiring paper, urging her colleagues to have more faith in the value of their emotional responses to patients on the basis that 'the counter-transference is an instrument of research into the patient's unconscious'.[15]

It is via the medium of the transference that the patient brings those aspects of early experience that need to be thought about to overcome their difficulties, but have been repressed or made inaccessible to consciousness because of the mental pain associated with them. They act upon them, rather than being able to remember them. Transference is memory expressed as interpersonal action. And thus configured, the transference is a particularly compact and complicated phenomenon: it leads to the reproduction of core problems (the way we see, in troubled people, the repetition of destructive interactions with others), as well as providing an extraordinarily effective communication of the nature of these problems. It conveys despair, often bringing about stuck patterns of relating, and also hope, in that through it the patient gives the therapist a real and immediate sense of their difficulties.

Of course, it is the way in which the communication is received – whether in a spirit of stasis or of hope and belief in the possibility of understanding – that makes the difference.

The transference is an immediate and often intensely experienced form of symbolic thinking, although it is seldom recognised as such since by definition it is felt to have the status of an unquestionable fact, a product of the here-and-now relationship between patient and therapist and nothing else. It is then one of the principle tasks of the therapy to explore the associative links which constitute the transference. The desired shift is from the concrete to the symbolic. The transference reaction does not necessarily disappear, but the aim is to make the patient aware of key figures that feature in their internal drama, and the symbolic connections they use in giving meaning to current experience.

Along with other forms of symbolic or associative thinking thrown up by the unconscious mind – dreams, jokes, slips of the tongue – the transference works in contradictory ways. It both wants to be known about and does not want to be known about. (There is something paradoxical about the suggestion that the unconscious mind has any sense of conscious agency, but here we are up against the limits of language.) It presents an opportunity to deal with a problem area because with it the patient brings to the therapist what is often the core, underlying difficulty in a particularly vivid and full form; but it also presents itself in such a way so as to mask the real nature of the problem.

It is all too easy to fall into a reductive view of transference, one in which past experiences of important figures are projected onto the blank screen of the therapist and the therapeutic situation. In this configuration, the therapist simply becomes someone else in the mind of the patient and a straightforward substitution takes place. But we are all, I hope, better artists than that. Lakoff and Johnson's landmark book about the everyday use of metaphor comes to mind.[16] It gives an account of how, when two disparate objects are brought together by association, new possibilities emerge for exploring the qualities of both (for example, the cheese-like quality of the moon and the shiny brightness of freshly made cheese) and other qualities are obscured by the link (the blue of the moon, the yellow of the cheese), hidden by the particular connection the mind has made over and above other connections.

As a therapist, it is very helpful to explore the symbolic workings of the mind in this way — as exposing and masking different aspects of the people that it has mentally taken in and represented to and for itself, driven by the dynamic relationship between what is conscious and unconscious at any one point in time.

The psychoanalytic narrative, and particularly the theory of transference, can be viewed as tragic, spoiling the ideal of true, objective relations between humans. This is how people react to the ideas when they first encounter them, before they have learnt in any depth about the potential of the therapeutic relationship to make use of unconscious communication and the way in which a human being in distress or difficulty can use another human being to help them understand themselves. But in the end, as I see it, psychoanalysis provides a compelling theory of human interrelatedness, a theory of relationships that emphasises how people feel things on behalf of others, how people need other people to understand, and indeed in order to learn to be, themselves.

It tells, I think, of the creative value of confusion. It is a comic narrative, in fact, of the best sort.

ELEVEN

An ideal society as one in which the citizens' fictions of themselves magically mesh one with another. Phenomenology of reading. The relationship between writer and reader as interior dialogue. Perils of amateur psychotherapy in the classroom. What the teacher can learn from psychoanalysis.

W. G. Sebald on the nature of personal and historical truth. His novel Austerlitz. *The struggles of the character Austerlitz to grasp his historical identity. Sebald as corrective to the notion that we are free to invent ourselves and others. The emphasis in psychoanalysis on self-understanding as work in progress. The paradox in Sebald that limitations of vision may lead to more intense insight.*

The efforts of young Austerlitz to forget (repress) the trauma of his separation from his parents and his past. The puzzle of why the adult Austerlitz does not seek help in psychoanalysis. The role of the narrator in giving form to Austerlitz's past. The return of the repressed and the stake of the novel as genre in insisting on the inevitability of this return.

❖

JMC – You say that it is comical that we spend our lives groping toward self-understanding via one misplaced identification after another. Maybe; but isn't it tragic too that our progress has to be so comically blind and halting?

You and I are reaching full circle in our exchanges. Your faith seems undimmed that we can learn to 'be ourselves'. Would that it were so simple, I say to myself. To my mind, it will be enough if we can settle on fictions of ourselves which we can inhabit more or less comfortably, fictions that interact sans friction with the fictions of those around us. In fact, that would be my notion of a good society, even an ideal society: one in which, for each of us, our fiction (our fantasy) of ourself goes unchallenged; and where some grand Leibnizian presiding force sees to it that all the billions of personal fictions interlock seamlessly, so that none of us need stay awake at night wondering anxiously whether the world we inhabit is real.

I recently happened to hear a talk by the actress Juliette Binoche during which she said (courageously, it seemed to me) that when she makes a film, her relationship with the director needs to be an erotic one – if not, the work will suffer. She hastened to add that she did not mean that they have to go to bed together. But the actress has to be ready to give herself up to the director, to be at one with his vision; and vice versa. She did not elaborate further, but whether consciously or not she was clearly recalling Plato's position on the relation between teacher and acolyte: that the energies tapped into in teaching and learning are those of Eros.

The theory of transference and counter-transference helps us – and by us I here mean not you and me, the outsiders, the commentators, but the couple who have voluntarily embarked on the process – to understand in a conscious way what is going on in the room (the consulting room, the acting studio, the classroom).

In the classroom what goes on is, of course, teaching and learning; but the idea of learning, it seems to me, assumes its full human meaning only when it includes grasping how it is that I am coming-to-understand. That is why I am so sceptical of distance learning – learning from a teacher who is not aware of my specific, individual existence. I am not claiming that distance teaching can achieve nothing at all. There may be a transfer of knowledge; there may even be, for the student, illumination. But as learning the activity remains truncated. The quintessential experience of learning, which is a feeling of growing beyond yourself, of leaving your old self behind and becoming a new, better self, and is a form of ecstasy or ek-stasis, either does not occur or, when it occurs, leaves you hanging in the air.

Of course the question at once arises: If distance learning is always an incomplete way of learning, what about reading? Don't books come to us from a distance? Can we not learn from books? Does reading really leave one hanging in the air?

I don't want to stray too far from the topic, but reading seems to demand a phenomenological analysis of its own. There is a dead reading and a living reading. Dead reading, in which the words never come alive on the page, is the experience of many children, those children who never, as they say, learn to love reading. It is not impossible to learn by means of dead reading, in a rote kind of way; but in itself it is a barren, unappealing experience. Living reading, on the other hand, strikes me as a mysterious affair. It involves finding one's way into the voice that speaks from the page, the voice of the Other, and inhabiting that voice, so that you speak to yourself (your self) from outside yourself. The process is thus a dialogue of sorts, though an interior one. The art of the writer, an art that is nowhere to be studied though it can be picked up, lies in creating a shape (a phantasm capable of speech), and an entry point that will allow the reader to inhabit the phantasm.

(Analogous to the dialogue between the reader and the reader's fiction of the writer, in living reading, is the dialogue between the writer and the writer's fiction of the reader that belongs to the experience of writing. That is to say, someone, some phantasm of the reader, is spoken to and speaks back as the words go down on the page.)

You are very strict, very professional (in the sense of guarding the integrity of the profession), in your condemnation of the teacher who practises amateur psychotherapy in the classroom, and I am sure you are right. The student is in a vulnerable position. If the teacher doesn't know what he or she is doing, the student can emerge confused and damaged. But the lesson to draw is not that a little knowledge – in this case a little knowledge of psychoanalytic theory – is a dangerous thing. The lesson lies elsewhere.

Think of the latter of the two cases I described earlier, the case of the student who, through slavishly imitating the teacher, learns nothing. The tendency of many teachers, encountering a student of this kind, is to point out to the student that they have failed to understand that they are required to demonstrate intellectual independence, an ability to produce ideas of their own; and then, when a few half-hearted ideas are produced and argued without conviction, to conclude that the student is second-rate material, and switch off.

Here the teacher may fail to see – indeed, may not regard it as in their remit to see – why, at a human, psychological level, the student is doing a mechanical imitation of learning rather than actually learning. To correct the student – to put it more accurately, to lead them out of the impasse in which they find themself – calls for more thought and pedagogical skill than merely explaining to them where they have gone wrong and telling them to do better next time. It may require spending time with them, undirected time, letting them talk about this, that and the other, letting them see that their thoughts interest you even though you may not happen to agree with them. In the parlance of some educators this might be called confidence building, but I don't think that is a correct analysis. What you are doing is allowing the student to engage with you more fully at a human level and thus to build up a less phantastical, more complicated, and (one hopes) truer picture of the figure with whom they will be engaging in dialogue when they write their next paper.

Does such an approach 'work', in the sense of correcting the student's 'problem'? Of course not. The 'problem' of dependency can't be solved in a half-hour chat. But maybe, five or ten years later, in the course of mulling over the past, the person whom the student will have become will begin to see why the professor in the course in which they fared so poorly was so inexplicably friendly; and maybe that moment, that insight, will constitute the true (if belated) learning experience.

Giving time to a student, seemingly contentless time, is not exactly therapy, professional or otherwise. It neither cures the student of whatever was 'wrong' with them, nor does it do the job of transforming a 'poor' student into a 'good' one. But it isn't exactly pedagogics either, not if the spirit in which the time is given is a Freudian one, by which I mean that it doesn't suffer from the delusion that the only two parties in the room are the teacher and the student, the teacher 'themself' and the student 'themself'. In Freudian space one is always accompanied by ghosts from the past.

☙

AK – I would like, by way of an ending, to turn to the work of W. G. Sebald, and specifically to his novel *Austerlitz*, which was published just before he died in a car accident in his late fifties. For if Dostoevsky should be read by all who have cause to think about the potential complexities involved in the act of soul-baring, Sebald is a resource for anyone – psychotherapist or otherwise – concerned with our main theme, the theme to which we keep returning: the nature of personal and historical truth.

The central character, Austerlitz (which turns out not to be his real name), is in his essence mysterious, unknown and unknow-able – as much to himself as to other people. What we do learn about him and his personal history (which is intimately connected with the history of the Second World War) we learn through his encounters and conversations with a narrator, about whom we know very little. In reading this book one can have the mistaken impression that one is steadily and gradually getting to know the man Austerlitz. But of course Austerlitz is always mediated through the figure of the narrator, who draws attention to the way in which he studies and approaches Austerlitz as a central character by telling us, for example, about making notes after long conversations so as to forget as little as possible, pointing to the fact that Austerlitz only in the end exists as an elaborate construction (of Sebald's, of the narrator's, of the reader's), which tells us as much about our own fantasies and identifications and preoccupations as the factual history of a man caught up in the dramatic events of mid-twentieth-century middle Europe.

What we are told by Austerlitz, via the narrator, is that during the Second World War when he was five his parents sent him away from Czechoslovakia on the *Kindertransport*. He was brought up in Wales by a Calvinist couple who called him by the name of David Elias and told him nothing of his early life. The stories reported by Austerlitz to the narrator largely concern the retrieval of his childhood memories from both before and after he left Czechoslovakia, and they are as much about the process of research and retrieval as they are about historical places and events.

Your comments about the teaching relationship bring to mind a particular passage of the book in which Austerlitz describes a history teacher at primary school who notices his talent and his curiosity about history and goes on to become an influential friend and mentor. The teacher, André Hilary, accompanies Austerlitz on visits to houses in Oxfordshire of historical interest and Austerlitz goes on to study at the same Oxford college as Hilary and to become an architectural historian.

Austerlitz, who is in the grip of a real crisis of identity, certainly adopts the vision of his teacher, but this is in part a regressive move, taking him even further away from a true sense of himself than he was before. Austerlitz is given a second false name by the headmaster of the school (he becomes at this point 'Austerlitz' and not 'David Elias') and Hilary supplies the name with grand historical meaning through his dramatic enactments in front of the class of the Battle of Austerlitz, which took place during the Napoleonic wars. This gives Austerlitz the very pleasing sense of being connected to France's grand and self-aggrandising imperial past, but of course this past is very far removed from his Czechoslovakian Jewish heritage.

Now, with the help of Sebald, I will respond to one of your frustrations with the psychoanalytic vision, or at least my version of it, and in particular the sense of the limitations of human knowledge and agency it articulates and the weight given by it to unconscious over conscious knowledge. I think from your point of view it is unfortunate that there are such heavy constraints on our knowledge about ourselves and other people, and that we have to struggle and work to the extent we do at developing what little real knowledge and understanding we have. I can certainly sympathise. But one can turn the matter on its head and take the view that it is both a surprise and a pleasure that we manage to see or understand as much as we do, given our place in the overall scheme of things. And Sebald helps take this line of thinking further, giving narrative form to the notion that it is not *despite* our frailties and blind spots and infirmities – both physical and mental – that we engage in acts of comprehension and insight, but *because* of them.

Images of fog, mist and twilight abound in *Austerlitz*, so that the impression gained is of a journey of discovery in which the colours and characters of history, both on the European main stage and in Austerlitz's early life, emerge out of the darkness. They are framed by it, and shine all the brighter because of it. The novel is littered with descriptions of physical infirmity, to the extent that one can pretty much guarantee that before hearing about any act of creative, intellectual or physical endeavour one will learn about the illness or disability or, at the very least, the extreme discomfort of the artist or intellectual or actor in question. There are some amusing descriptions of eye problems in the early part of the book. The narrator, about whom, as I said, we know next to nothing, does manage to tell us about a visit to the ophthalmologist just before meeting Austerlitz for the first time; and when he sees him again after a period of twenty years he catches sight of him – of course – at the periphery of his vision.

What is the message I take from *Austerlitz*? It is this: that of course we all have limitations and infirmities aplenty, weaknesses and blind spots which shape and contort what we are able to see of ourselves and of the world around us. And what is perhaps remarkable is not that we are constrained in our sights, but that we have insight into anything at all. Indeed, understanding something of who we are and of our context is to some extent contingent on relinquishing the aspiration to perfect vision. Knowledge – at least of the type in which Sebald is interested – is gained by letting go of mastery as an aim.

There is a lovely detail in the book that illustrates this: the narrator tells us about female opera singers of the past who used to apply drops of belladonna to their eyes, which then shone on stage with a clarity and radiance that belied the fact that they could not see anything at all. The belladonna briefly blinded them, and the appearance produced by it of complete and perfect sight, of shining eyes that communicate heightened identity and understanding to the audience, masked a state of real temporary infirmity. By contrast, if one relaxes the urge for mastery and intellectual control, one does become more open to certain kinds of stimulation and insight – particularly in the emotional and creative spheres.

As an artist, you must know all about this. It is yet another point at which the paths of creativity and psychotherapeutic process converge.

⁂

JMC – Thank you for introducing *Austerlitz* into our discussion. Sebald didn't like to call his books novels, but *Austerlitz* is clearly a novel and, what is more, one of the major novels of recent times. In the context of Sebald's life I see it as a work in progress, a project in coming to terms with history that was not yet completed at the time when he wrote its inconclusive last pages. Thus I see the book as more troubled than you do, and certainly not confident about offering us wisdom or guidance.

Despite my admiration for it, I confess I have struggled with *Austerlitz* in the past and still struggle with it. The density of its texture threatens to overwhelm me, as I suppose the density of the texture of the world threatens to overwhelm 'Austerlitz' himself. But the action of the novel is clear and simple enough, or at least seems so. A small boy is brought up in Wales by a couple named Elias; he goes by the name Dafydd or David Elias. He is sent to boarding school, where at a certain point he is told that his real name is Jacques Austerlitz. Later he will discover that this too is not his real name: his father's name was Aychenwald. And there, more or less, the book ends: with 'Austerlitz' trying to learn more about Aychenwald, who perished in the Holocaust.

In my summary, the action commences not in Czechoslovakia (where Elias/Austerlitz/Aychenwald was born) but in Wales; and it commences there because the boy has forgotten or made himself forget Czechoslovakia. He continues to forget his origins until he is in his thirties, when a strange crisis occurs: he has a vision of a child sitting in the waiting room at a London railway station, and realises that the child is himself. This vision precipitates a mental collapse that includes loss of memory. He is hospitalised for a lengthy period, and only 'becomes himself' again after therapy consisting of soothing, repetitive work in a horticultural nursery.

Towards the end of the book he will have another collapse, in Paris. This time he will be brought back by reading and rereading a little manual of herbal cures for forms of spiritual distress, dating from the eighteenth century.

I come to the first point I want to make. 'Austerlitz' is suffering from something, and the first approximation we can give to the name of what afflicts him is repression, a strategy for defending himself against an intolerable past. He was not unhappy being Dafydd Elias, as for a while thereafter he was not unhappy being Jacques Austerlitz, but that integument of ordinary happiness – of just being a normal person – cannot hold out against the weight of memory dammed up inside him. Memory bursts out in the waiting room, and (presumably) the effort of repressing it again results in the paralysis of his first collapse.

'Austerlitz' has suffered the psychic trauma of being wrenched without warning or explanation from his parents and his language and his place of birth, and consigned to the care of cold strangers in a foreign land (Wales). At a deeper level, he is suffering from the trauma of surviving in a kind of half-aware state while his family and Middle European Jewry in general have been extinguished. At a personal level (as a boy) and at a symbolic level (as a survivor of the Holocaust) he needs help, therapy. Psychoanalytic psychotherapy would seem to be tailor-made for him. Nor, living in the London of the 1960s, would he have lacked for resources. Yet there is no mention of psychoanalysis in the book. The two cures that 'Austerlitz' finds are pointedly homely, practical, not rooted in any theory of the psyche. One cannot help inferring that Sebald intends something by this: that if there is any cure for the Austerlitzian condition, it will not be provided by psychoanalysis. My guess is that psychoanalysis cannot (in the view of Sebald the writer) offer aid because psychoanalysis is ahistorical (I must add that I have no knowledge of what Sebald the man thought of psychoanalysis).

What 'Austerlitz' does not want to remember is, of course, that the railway waiting room was a staging point in his journey, at the age of four and as a refugee from the Nazis, from his home in Prague to the Welsh valleys and the Dafydd Elias identity. And, as you point out, the second collapse is connected with the collapse of the second fiction, the fiction of the Jacques Austerlitz identity, which he has connected since his schooldays – irrelevantly – with the Battle of Austerlitz in 1805. For insofar as his name is Austerlitz he is connected not with Napoleonic heroics but with the more mundane Gare d'Austerlitz in Paris and its association with the massive appropriation, cataloguing, and disposal of the goods of the murdered Jews of France.

So my second point – a somewhat peripheral one – is that the history teacher who so inspires him, Hilary, actually misleads him by pointing him to the wrong place to look for his origins, or at least the origin of his name. Hilary teaches him false history.

The third point I would want to make goes back to my remark about being overwhelmed, as reader, by *Austerlitz*. What threatens to overwhelm me in the book, namely its torrent of detail, is also what threatens the mental stability of 'Austerlitz'. Once the wound, the trauma, is reopened, one can drown in what pours out.

'Austerlitz' controls the torrent of memory (memory in the widest sense, including the historical memory of Europe) by turning it, as far as he can, into a narrative with a recognisable chronology or set of chronologies (the narrative of his life; the narrative of his historical researches; the narrative of his mother's life, insofar as that is recoverable; and so forth). That is to say, 'Austerlitz' mimics what Sebald does when he creates a man (unnamed) who meets a man named Austerlitz who, in a series of chapter-like bursts, tells him his story.

So we come to the question of the formal structure of the book, and specifically the question of the narrator. Why is a narrator necessary? Why could the narration not simply have been done by 'Austerlitz'?

The answer is of course that the narrator is not a Jew. Specifically, the narrator is a German non-Jew, more or less a contemporary of 'Austerlitz', living by choice in England. It would be silly to say that this man does not know 'about' the Holocaust. But the story we read in *Austerlitz* is the story of a man being told the story of the Holocaust – more specifically, a story of trying and failing to repress the Holocaust, of trying and failing to put it (pack it away) in the history books. To the extent that the Holocaust is not part of the living present of the narrator, 'Austerlitz' is the narrator's repressed, a repressed that returns to haunt him.

Thus we arrive at my final point, which connects Austerlitz with questions I was raising at the beginning of our dialogue. The dramatic arc of the narrative of 'Jacques Austerlitz' consists of repression followed by crisis followed by revelation of the truth. But why does 'Austerlitz' have the initial crisis, the vision in the waiting room at Liverpool Street station? Why does he have to have it?

The banal answer is that the vision sets his quest in motion, and without that quest we would have no book. (In the first pages of the first novel we have in English, Robinson Crusoe asks himself why we can't be satisfied with just sliding comfortably through life, why we have to go out into the world and risk ourselves, why we are driven to become 'instruments of our own destruction'. The question is as old as the novel itself, perhaps as old as storytelling: it sets storytelling in motion.)

The deeper answer to my question of why 'Austerlitz' has his vision, the answer on which Sebald's book is predicated, is that what is repressed returns.

My further question then is: What if the repressed does not always return? What if, for every young Dafydd/Jacques under whose feet the stories that have sustained him collapse, there is another Dafydd/Jacques who never agonises about who he really is but slides comfortably through life, wrapped in the stories he has been told about himself?

It is of no use to argue that the countless instances we have of the repressed returning to haunt us prove that the repressed always returns, since by definition we don't hear of cases where the repressed does not return.

It is hard, perhaps impossible, to make a novel that is recognisably a novel out of the life of someone who is from beginning to end comfortably sustained by fictions. We make a novel only by exposing those fictions. As a genre the novel seems to have a constitutional stake in the claim that things are not as they seem to be, that our seeming lives are not our real lives. And psycho-analysis, I would say, has a comparable stake.

REFERENCES

1. For a fuller account of Melanie Klein's ideas on the paranoid-schizoid and depressive positions the reader is directed to Chapters 2 and 5 of Hanna Segal, *Introduction to the Work of Melanie Klein* (London: William Heinemann, 1964).

2. Neville Symington, 'The analyst's act of freedom as an agent of therapeutic change', in *International Journal of Psycho-Analysis* (1983), vol. 10 no. 3, pp. 283–91.

3. The reader is directed to the account of Wilfred Bion's theory of containment in Chapter 16 of James Grotstein, *A Beam of Intense Darkness: Wilfred Bion's Legacy* (London: Karnac Books, 2007).

4. Hanna Segal, 'Reflections on Truth, Tradition and the Psychoanalytic Tradition of Truth', in *Imago* (2006), vol. 63 no. 3, pp. 283–92.

5. Isabel Menzies Lyth, 'Social systems as a defence against anxiety: An empirical study of the nursing service of a general hospital', in *Human Relations* (1960), vol. 13, pp. 95–121.

6. D. H. Lawrence, 'Fenimore Cooper's White Novels', in *Studies in Classic American Literature* (New York: Viking, 1964), pp. 35–6.

7. Isabel Menzies Lyth, 'A Psychoanalytical Perspective on Social Institutions', in Eric Trist and Hugh Murray (eds), *The Social Engagement of Social Science, Volume 1, The Social-Psychological Perspective*(London: Free Association Books, 1990), pp. 463–75.

8. W. R. Bion, *Experiences in Groups* (London: Tavistock, 1961).

9. Eugène N. Marais, *The Soul of the White Ant* (London, 1938) and *The Soul of the Ape* (London, 1973). The former book appeared first as a series of articles in Afrikaans periodicals between 1923 and 1925. The latter, unfinished at the time of Marais' death in 1936, was published posthumously.

10. *The Report of the Mid-Staffordshire NHS Foundation Trust Public Inquiry*, 6 February 2013.

11. Ronald Britton, 'The missing link: parental sexuality in the Oedipus complex', in Ronald Britton, Michael Feldman and Edna O'Shaughnessy (eds), *The Oedipus Complex Today: Clinical Implications* (London: Karnac Books, 1989).

12. Thomas Nagel, 'What is it like to be a bat?' (1974), in *Mortal Questions* (Cambridge: Cambridge University Press, 1991), pp. 164–79.

13. Donald Winnicott, 'Ego Distortion in Terms of True and False Self', in *The Maturational Process and the Facilitating Environment* (London: Hogarth Press, 1995), and Donald Winnicott, *Playing and Reality* (London: Routledge, 1971).

14. Anne Alvarez, 'Play and the imagination: where pathological play may demand a more intensified response from the therapist', in *The Thinking Heart: Three levels of psychoanalytic therapy with disturbed children* (London: Routledge, 2012).

15. Paula Heimann, 'On Counter-Transference', in *International Journal of Psychoanalysis* (1950), vol. 31, pp. 81–4.

16. George Lakoff and Mark Johnson, *Metaphors We Live By* (Chicago: University of Chicago Press, 1980).

GLOSSARY

Defences or defence mechanisms

These are general terms to describe the ways in which the human mind reacts in order to protect itself from psychic pain. Such pain then remains partly or entirely unconscious. The type of defence used will depend upon the person's developmental stage, character and constitution, as well as on the nature and extent of the mental distress they are trying to modify or provide an escape from. Defences may be used for a while and then reduced or dropped when they are no longer needed, in which case they serve to protect and promote developmental processes. Alternatively, they can be clung to even when they are no longer useful, in which case they can hinder or obstruct forward movement.

Introjection

Introjection is a mental process whereby a significant person or thing is taken inside the self, either in whole or in part. Introjection can be a useful way of drawing on a positive relationship or influence, or it may represent an unhealthy defence against separation anxiety and loss. The model is of bodily incorporation: what is taken in is, so to speak, swallowed, absorbed, and made part of the self.

Oedipal situation or Oedipus complex

In modern psychoanalytic thinking, the Oedipal situation refers to the point in childhood development when the exclusivity of a two-person relationship is relinquished and the child can begin to relate to, and allow for the reality of, the parental couple. The Oedipal situation is universal and not dependent on the context of the nuclear family. At first the child wishes to possess their mother or main carer completely. But at a certain stage in optimal development, the fact of the mother's exclusive attachment to the father (or to something of her own – another person or activity) is brought home to them. If the mother's need and desire for her own adult relationship or activity is not accepted, the child's development is obstructed, holding them back within a cross-generational couple and making it difficult for them to form an independent sexual identity or to relate to intimates in a secure way during adulthood.

According to Freudian psychology, the Oedipus complex is experienced most intensely during the phallic stage of development, from the ages of three to five, and declines during the so-called latency period. It returns at full force during puberty, and its successful resolution is measured by the extent to which the person is able to separate from their parents to form their own identity, choosing sexual partners and enjoying a sexual life as an autonomous individual.

Patient-offender
The term used to refer to a person who has been convicted of a criminal offence but has been sent by the court for treatment within a secure mental-health facility rather than to prison to serve a custodial sentence.

Projection
Projection is a form of primitive defence whereby feelings that a person does not want to recognise as an aspect of themselves are got rid of by locating them in another person or thing. It is a common psychic strategy, employed by all of us in some degree. In clinical form it is seen in phobias, where unbearable negative feelings are disowned and relocated outside the self, and in paranoia. Projection can be productive when there is sympathetic

communication between the person doing the projecting and the person receiving it, such that it then becomes possible for disowned feelings to be recognised as part of the self.

Reality principle

According to Freud, the reality principle regulates mental functioning alongside its counterpart, the pleasure principle. The reality principle controls and modifies the innate drive for pleasure in response to the demands of the outside world. The ego is the part of the mind that negotiates between the dictates of external reality and the urge for pleasure.

Regression

Regression is a return to an earlier point in one's psychic history or development. Insofar as the psychotherapeutic situation may trigger memories of vulnerability and dependence during childhood, regression is a natural response, and helpful to the therapist, since it opens the patient to the experience of therapy and often marks an unconscious return to the particular stage in life where they had difficulty. However, it can be obstructive when a patient becomes stuck in a regressed mode of functioning.

Repetition compulsion

The repetition compulsion describes the tendency of the human mind to repeat unconscious traumatic experience, often from early in development, in a bid for conscious control and mastery. Thus, problematic childhood relationships tend to recur in adulthood, usually in disguised form, and it may be the case that such unconscious repetition will be overcome only if and when the individual becomes able to understand the true source and nature of the difficulty.

Repression

Repression is the prototypical defensive process, in which the memories, thoughts and feelings that are attached to an instinct are pushed into the realm of the unconscious because of their threatening or disturbing nature. The instinct then returns, but in a disguised form. Repression is a universal form of defence and is integral to the development of the unconscious as a major part of the psyche. The term is often used synonymously with defence in general, and does indeed play a part in many other defensive processes.

Resistance
The term applied to any element of the words and actions of the patient that serves to obstruct awareness of unconscious feelings and motivations. Resistance is often itself unconscious. Resistance can be manifested in the form of internal defences, emerging in the way the patient presents themselves in therapy, or of external behaviours. Both of these function to ensure that the patient does not need to face up to something that feels unbearably painful.

Social defence system
A system of defences within an organisation or social group which develops over a period of time and often manifests itself within what is thought of as the neutral area of the group's customary practices. The system functions to protect individuals from psychic pain or discomfort. Yet without facing up to such pain, the group – and this is particularly true of human services – may find that its efforts to carry out its tasks are undermined from within.

Splitting
Splitting is a primitive form of defence: a person or object is perceived in divided, black-and-white terms because acknowledgment of a more complex and ambivalent response would threaten the individual's sense of identity. In a typical case a figure important to the individual is presented in strongly positive terms (the figure is *idealised*), even though negative feelings may seep through, causing distress and dismay. As long as these

negative feelings are disowned, the split persists, allowing an idealised but unrealistic relationship to be maintained.

Superego
In Freud's model of the mind, the superego is the agency responsible for conscience and moral functioning. The formation of ideals, and the operation of restraints and prohibitions, are among the activities of the superego. Within Freudian orthodoxy the superego has been seen as the product of the Oedipal phase, resulting from the internalisation of parental prohibition. But many now think that it is formed earlier, or at least that there are psychological mechanisms in place from infancy that lay down the foundations for later superego development. From a clinical point of view it is useful to distinguish between a harsh superego, which sits in rather critical judgment over the rest of the personality and can be experienced as belittling and discouraging, and a more benign superego, which acts as a motivating and guiding force.

Transference
Transference is an unconscious process whereby feelings from early formative relationships are redirected onto somebody in the present – in the case of psychotherapy, onto the person of the psychotherapist. Transference reactions are a feature of everyday life but tend to develop a particular force in the therapeutic relationship because this relationship may trigger childhood memories of vulnerability in the face of difficulty and distress. Transference reactions are defensive in nature, in that they protect the individual from painful knowledge of the source and real nature of their feelings. They are particularly useful in psychoanalysis because they form a rich and immediate source of information about early relationships, to which there would otherwise be little or no access. Working through the transference relationship, that is, understanding its nature and resolving it in favour of a more reality-based relationship, is a major part of the task of psychoanalytic psychotherapy.